Simply the **BST** Crime Survival

A revolutionary self-defense plan rooted in LOVE and COURAGE!

A healing blend of HEART-TALK and simple, explicit street fighting designed specifically for NICE PEOPLE!

Debbie Gardner

"Most *Dangerous* Woman in America"

Simply the BST ... Crime Survival

To contact the PUBLISHER:
BookMasters, Inc.
2541 Ashland Road, P.O. Box 2139
Mansfield, Ohio 44905
Phone 419-589-5100
Fax 419-589-4040
Sales 1-800-537-6727
Web www.bookmasters.com

ISBN 09712087-0-0

To contact the AUTHOR:
Debbie Gardner
SURVIVE INSTITUTE
7265 Kenwood Road, Suite 315
Cincinnati, Ohio 45236
Phone 513-791-7453
Fax 513-791-7453
Email debbiegardner@surviveinstitute.com
Web www.surviveinstitute.com

Credits

Typesetting: Jaclyn Gardner
Proofreading: Mike Gardner, Jody Howells, Jaclyn Gardner
Front Cover Design: Nancy Gara
Front Cover Art: Nancy Gara
Back Cover Design: Marion Allman
Photos: Mike Gardner, Fred Thoman, David Doyle, Tom Herbert
Graphics: Mike Gardner, Jaclyn Gardner, Fred Thoman

ACKNOWLEDGEMENTS

I've given birth to *children* and birth to *books*, I believe books are more difficult! My family has been most gracious showering me with love, encouragement, creativity, fast food and patience during both my creative and *irritating* writing periods. Thanks to you all for your countless sacrifices!

MIKE, my husband - Etched in my memory is the metaphoric challenge you gave me to create SURVIVE INSTITUTE in 1982: "You be the *cover* and I'll be the ***spine*** ... A change is needed. If not you, Debbie ... who?" You are so much more than my professional ***spine!*** You are the ***air*** I breathe, you mean ***everything*** to me! Your daring, creative commitment to me ... and society is a priceless gift.

JACLYN, our extraordinary daughter - You brilliantly edited and typeset this book and it's *quadzillion* changes without losing your cool. Your quiet confidence and hard work stabilized me during rough times more than you know. You have proven what I have always known ... *"you can accomplish ANYTHING, SUPERwoman!"* Selfless devotion to your "*Mother's project"* was a "test" beyond the call of duty! I am indebted to you for not just caring about me, but my *life's purpose.* Your loving personality allowed me the freedom to create a business and *save lives ...* during your childhood.

JIMMY, our precious son - The "author" is gone and your "Mother" is back! ***Yes!*** For all the meals you learned to cook for yourself ... thanks ... you are an *independent* man now! Your comic relief and non-stop ball games were welcome interruptions that kept me sane when I was on hidden overload. I remain *stunned* at the keen insights on life you have offered me. You have grown up to be a focused, deep thinking, gentle, caring young man like your Father. Wow!

JOANNE GRUETTER, Producer – Your persistence and determination to get my **BST** message on Public Television was heroic. Because of you, countless lives will be saved. I treasure your *patience* with me. You are a true PRO!

WCET-48 MANAGEMENT & PRODUCTION Professionals-(Cincinnati, OH) I am honored by your support and membership in your "WCET family." You all put your *hearts* and *souls* into everything you do *and it shows* in your quality productions! Your work *matters!*

JODY HOWELLS (and Dave) – Thank you for years of behind the scenes support and encouragement! Your suggested changes in the book were right … and *awesome!*

NANCY GARA – Your gift of the *hands and heart* image adapted for my book cover is a *grand slam!* How can I thank you for visually capturing the essence of my life-time beliefs?

MARION ALLMAN, Art Institute of Cincinnati – You threw the *rock* that created so many wonderful waves of creative ideas that visually impacted my life. Thank you for your help with the back book cover!

CULLEN HANLON, VP Corporate Security, KELLY SERVICES - Thank you for your decade-long, worldwide support & for printing over a *hundred thousand* classy, color handouts for my seminar audiences! They are treasured by ALL who have received them!

CURT SELLERS & KEITH MEYERS of Curtis, Inc – Your partnership in our "YES YOU CAN *SURVIVE"* video has helped us spread our message around the world. THANK YOU!

SURVIVE INSTITUTE CLIENTS and GRADUATES! My mission *thrives* because of your investment in me, and *word of mouth* endorsements *behind my back!* Your consistent support and feedback keeps me *electrified. Thank you so much!*

ALL GARDNER and HERBERT FAMILY MEMBERS – My foundation is solid because my roots are *deep* and *healthy.* For years, you have ALL *been there* … ready, willing and able to help Mike and I accomplish our creative ventures. You are the "net" that gives us the courage to keep moving forward. We love you ALL … and vow to tell you more often.

CONTENTS

FOREWORD

Lessons from a "Reformed" Wimp

"Get in the "_" alley and get your clothes off!"

A drug-crazed man jumped from behind a building, and said those words to me as he shoved a gun in my stomach. I was walking to my car from a restaurant with two male friends. Hundreds of hours of martial arts training, police self-defense courses and near perfect grades in college didn't help ... ***I FROZE!***

My friends instantly took control! They pushed the gun and gunman into a wall. The gun broke when it hit the ground. It was a TOY gun. What appeared to be so dangerous, immediately became ridiculous. My attacker was a pitiful, intoxicated "street-person" rendered harmless within seconds.

My friends' reaction was awesome and mine was dreadful. When they took control, I *ran* across the street; *hid* behind a pole wide enough to cover my eyes (not my butt), *prayed* ... and *cried* hysterically! At the time of this attack, I was on a path to graduate as one of the *first* highly trained, *patrol women* in the U.S. This was my *first* test with stranger-violence. *Taxpayers ... can you imagine me, protecting YOU, in those early days?* I could not even take care of myself!

I was devastated! I was tested and ... **I LOST!** It was time to stop kidding myself. All those *near* perfect grades, karate belts and training certificates hanging on my wall meant *nothing.* When challenged, I could not transfer and apply my professional training from the *gym* ... to *reality.*

I decided to quit the police academy. Then a fellow cadet convinced me to stay. He said that my willingness to discuss fear was a sign of strength ... not weakness. He had a hunch that we were *over-trained,* and desperately lacked focus. I was so impressed with his on-target, heartwarming insights that I married him a year later.

With Mike's help, my failure served as a significant emotional event that motivated me to search past the complicated rhetoric of self-defense mis-information, and uncover the true principles for emotional, as well as physical control in a crisis. **A handful of simple principles saved my career and changed both of our lives.** Mike and I dared to believe a *new* idea for *realistic* self-defense:

*Less is **MORE,** when "less" is RIGHT!*

My training, research, life experiences and observations convinced me that most **law-abiding citizens, need and want *courage* for crisis survival and *memorable* self-defense choices.** However, most do not have the time, money, fitness, or interest in taking a traditional, complicated self-defense class. What a dilemma!

As a "reformed wimp" I realized a simple revolution in traditional self-defense education was necessary and long overdue. I identified this question as the challenge:

***"What can MOST people quickly learn to do,
...that will work MOST of the time,
...with little or NO PHYSICAL practice?"***

It has taken me 25 years to design my self-defense plan. Summarized by the letters **B-S-T,** I hope it provides many answers you have been searching for!

NOTES:

For easy reading, I have made a few choices:

1. *I use the pronoun "he" throughout the book when referring to a "criminal." I know women can be criminals too!*

2. ***RUNNING and ESCAPING*** *are always the best choice to prevent crime. The purpose of this book is to give you options when RUNNING and ESCAPING are not possible!*

3. *I spell "best" throughout the book as* ***BST*** *to regularly remind you of your crime survival summary ...* ***"B-S-T!"*** *This "positive annoyance" is a "memory technique!"*

4. *What I offer in this book are simple PRINCIPLES rather than a collection of complicated, memorized techniques.*

Do you remember third grade math?

You did not memorize all of the answers to every possible multiplication problem. Instead, you memorized formulas (principles) that quickly led to the answers.

"What lies behind us
and what lies before us
are tiny matters,
compared to what lies
within us."

Ralph Waldo Emerson

Chapter One

September 11th, 2001 ...

"FREEDOM is at war with FEAR!" President George W. Bush

... changed everything. Unthinkable terrorist attacks in the United States exploded the hearts of rational law-abiding citizens around the world. The need for updated personal safety, especially on an airplane, became an immediate priority worldwide!

The threat of continued terrorism, as well as the everyday fear of civilian violence, has caused people of all ages to feel a desperate need for realistic crime survival truths. Law abiding citizens have no time to "practice" complicated theories and techniques, and no interest in the clutter of "traditional safety fluff." The need today is to learn explicit truths *FAST* for possible *use SOON.*

How did 9-11-01 affect you? Did it leave you bitter or better? Scared? Motivated? Depressed? Fearful? Angry? Confused? Do you worry about the future world your family and children will live in?

"Worrying" is like "rocking" in a rocking chair. It takes a lot of energy, and always move you backwards!"

What is important during uncertain, unpredictable times is that you accept the only real control you have in life ... and that is ... CONTROL OF YOU!

Imagine a crisis where most people are empowered with SELF-CONTROL, then have the ability to reach over and help someone else!

Legally, morally and emotionally, I am going to help you become that *self-controlled* person who can at least TRY to survive ANY crisis, not just crime.

Starting NOW, decide that the FEAR of CRIME, especially TERRORISM is **not** going to destroy your quality of life. Decide that an abundance of moral courage and extraordinary natural power has always been *sleeping* inside of you, and is now about to be *awakened!*

Decide that your safety is YOUR responsibility ... 100% of the time. Yes, security, military, federal and local law enforcement officers are in position to help you be safe. Their job, however, is to *"get there"* not *"be there"* when a crime occurs. A lot can happen until you are "rescued." What specifically are you going to do to save yourself ... until your "back-up" arrives?

Debbie Gardner's Definition of
SELF DEFENSE:
Learning to CONTROL YOURSELF
so if tested, you can manipulate someone else
hopefully, in a NON-VIOLENT way.

Isn't it interesting?

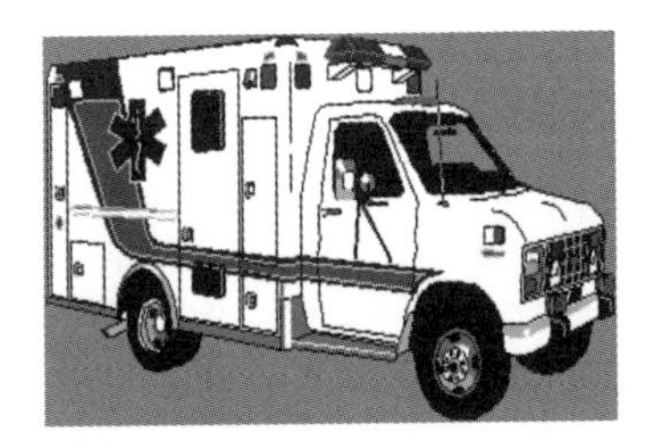

If a woman falls and breaks a leg in a parking lot, she doesn't expect the life-squad to BE THERE. As seconds pass, she knows she needs to do *minimum* FIRST AID to *save herself* until rescued.

However, if a woman is attacked by a criminal in a parking lot, somehow she expects the police or security to BE THERE **as the crime happens**. As seconds pass, she is stunned and later says: *"cops are never around when you need them."*

More than ever, our entire society (especially law enforcement) needs your help! Criminals need to *lose* and law-abiding citizens need to *win!* Learning to at least TRY to SAVE YOU is a priceless contribution with immeasurable benefits for our peace loving democracy.

Like the passengers and flight crew who fought terrorists on United Airlines Flight 93 ... that crashed in the fields of Pennsylvania instead of a public building ... never forget that your courageous, defensive actions might save the lives of others in ways no one ever dreamed possible.

"HEROES are not born
... they are cornered."

Chapter Two

Simple is B-S-T

Do you remember fourth grade fire safety?

" Stop! Drop! Roll!"

Although it is not enough data to qualify you to be a fire fighter, it is probably enough to help you *escape* or *survive* a fire until the fire department arrives!

You need an equally memorable crime prevention and survival plan. I suggest:

" B S T "

A complete explanation of each word follows in upcoming chapters. For now, just commit these trigger words to your memory:

B = Breathe!
S = Space!
T = Throat!

The full meaning behind the acronym **BST** is not enough data to qualify you to be a police officer, security guard, or karate master. Yet, **BST** may help you prevent or survive violence until a police officer arrives.

"FUNNELIZED" Self-Defense

My commitment to uncover a simple self-defense plan required a serious cut through non-essential data. It has taken decades of *teaching* ... then *testing the memory* of former students and audience members to feel confident in my **BST** summary. What a coincidence to discover that the first letter of each trigger word spelled ... **BeST!**

Upfront, I know that most people value my simplicity and agree with the **BST** summarized message. I also know *some* people, especially those who value or study complicated self-defense, will not be comfortable with the simplicity of **BST**! That is OK! Approval from *all* the people *all* the time is unrealistic and is not my goal.

> **My commitment is to create a simple message so that "MOST"** ... that large group of law-abiding citizens who are not formally trained and therefore tragically believe there is little or nothing they can do **... have a chance to save themselves.**

I am a *results-driven* person! I value your time, money and need for *immediate empowerment!* I want you to *feel better* immediately after experiencing my **BST** crime survival plan and I want you to share your new beliefs with everyone who will listen. (Going from *BST student* to *BST teacher* greatly enhances your life-time memory!) BEWARE! If you and I cross paths, I will test your memory ... because I need to know what you *caught* and *retained.* Most importantly, I want you to be able to choose from realistic tools if you are ever tested with violence.

Because I dared to ask for years of feedback, I have evidence that convinces me that MOST people can and do ***remember*** the **BST** crime survival plan.

Breathe
Scream
Gouge the eyes
Kick the groin
Stranger Danger
Never...
Go for the throat
Protect your space
Don't...
Always...
BST

Teaming up the WHAT's and WHY's

BST is your reminder of **what** specifically to do if attacked ... (**B**reathe! **S**pace! **T**hroat!) The **BST** plan provides *logical sense* and *memorable data* that goes directly into your HEAD.

A secondary acronym offered is **MVP** which explains ***why*** you have the right to defend yourself. In addition, it describes you as the **M**ost **V**aluable **P**layer in a crime survival scenario! In other words, the **MVP** explanation justifies *emotional data* for your HEART.

HEAD	HEART
B reathe triggers self control and ...	**M ental** righteous choices
S pace triggers crime prevention for ...	**V erbal** righteous choices
T hroat triggers crime survival for ...	**P hysical** righteous choices

When I tested people's resistance to many common self-defense choices, I made an interesting discovery that might apply to you.

Your ***head*** needs to know ***what!*** Your ***heart*** needs to justify ***why!*** In rapid crisis decision making, your *head* and *heart* need to ***agree*** before you are likely to take action.

> Example: If your *head* knows to *grab and twist the groin* in a ground fight, but your *heart* says, **"YUK, I can't or won't do that"** ... you probably can't and won't ... in a rapid attack.

I understand the importance of reaching your heart. It is my specialty! I will work hard to *gently* convince your heart to agree with uncomfortable crime survival concepts throughout the upcoming chapters.

THE MAGIC OF THREE

It's amazing how people have a better chance of committing data into *life-time* memory if the data is grouped in THREES. Remembering four items or more becomes a struggle.

MAGIC OF 3'S			PLAN OF ACTION for
A	B	C	
1	2	3	
Ready	Set	Go	*SPORTS*
Stop	Drop	Roll	*FIRE*
9	1	1	*EMERGENCY*
Check Airway	Stop Bleeding	Promote Circulation	*FIRST AID*
B	S	T	*SELF DEFENSE*

Example:
Emergency dialing used to be seven digits which was very difficult for people to remember in a crisis. *Simply dialing* ***9-1-1*** for the life squad, fire and police department is an enormous improvement that has saved countless lives!

I firmly believe that using only *three* letters to memorize self-defense WHAT's and WHY's is going to significantly help you *recall* and *react* effectively in a crisis.

Although taking time to consider ALL options is good in non-crisis decision-making, crime survival requires *split second* decision-making. **You don't have time!** Hesitation can lead to death! If there is a topic that needs to be taught simply, it is this one.

The science of "Hick's Law"[1] validates simplicity. It states that in **crisis decision making:** *"the fewer the choices, the more rapid the response."* It's more than a theory! Today there is actual scientific proof that:

LESS is ***MORE,*** when *"less" is RIGHT!*

[1] Motor Learning & Performance, Richard A Schmidt, UCLA.

DO I KNOW YOU?

You certainly know a lot about me. What about you?

Are you a survivor of crime?
Have you been threatened?
Are you in an emotionally abusive relationship?
Are you just sick and tired of being afraid?
Did a "bully" belittle you for the final time?
Are you researching for someone else?
Do you teach self-defense?
Are you in a physically abusive marriage?
Did a movie just scare you?
Are you curious about improved safety?
Did you just survive a *close call...*?

I guarantee my **BST** principles are going to help. Regardless of who you are and why you are reading, the bottom line is the **same** for everyone, regardless of your size, age, gender, academic background, and physical or emotional strengths.

Would you tolerate a course where the Red Cross taught CPR skills correctly to men ... then different, weaker skills to women and young adults? Of course not! You know effective life-saving CPR skills need to be taught the same to everyone.

SUMMARY of SIMPLE is BST!

Your life-saving plan is summarized by **B-S-T!**
Your right to defend yourself is summarized by **M-V-P!**

B = **B**reathe!
S = **S**pace!
T = **T**hroat!

M = **M**ental choices
V = **V**erbal choices
P = **P**hysical choices

Before further explaining the **BST** plan in depth, we need to strengthen your *emotional foundation* by turning sections of **"quicksand"** into "concrete."

*"The **BST angle** from which to solve a problem ... is the **TRY-angle**"*

I am only one; but still I am one.
I cannot do everything, but still I can do something;
I will not refuse to do the something I can do.
Helen Keller

Chapter Three

Foundation Repair

TURN "QUICKSAND" ... into "CONCRETE"

Answer these four questions courageously ...

1. Will violent crime exist throughout your lifetime? ***(... Yes!)***

2. Even though you are "careful and aware," do you admit that you could someday face unpreventable violence? ***(... "Yes!")***

3. At that exact moment in your life, who is 100% responsible for taking care of you? (...uncomfortable pause ... ***"ME!"***)

4. What do you *specifically* know to do to save your life, especially if your assailant is intoxicated and armed? (***"Not sure!" "Not much!" "NOTHING!"*** ...)

NOTHING! NOTHING!! NOTHING!!! When asked bluntly, too many law-abiding citizens admit they know **NOTHING SPECIFIC** to help them save their own life, especially against an armed, intoxicated assailant! How do I know? I ASK! Typical answers are in parenthesis above!

Each time I hear the response "**NOTHING!**" my blood boils and my passion for this subject soars! The time has come to publicly challenge conventional wisdom. Clearly, most crime prevention rhetoric is not connecting with the needs of law abiding citizens! Maybe it is time to THROW AWAY the majority of those well-intended crime prevention handouts filled with generic data.

Don't get me wrong. The professionals who write, distribute and teach generic "safety tips" and "self-defense" ideas are decent, caring people. Their generic message is not totally wrong, it's just totally out-of-date for today's needs... especially in times of terrorism and serious crime waves.

You and other law-abiding citizens already know the importance of generic "awareness" comments. In fact, you have heard them so much that you are sick of hearing them ... and still afraid. What you want and rarely hear ... is the emphasis of your RIGHTS as well as specific survival choices if your **BST** awareness and prevention isn't enough!

Not only do you want and need righteous, backbone-straightening choices, so does our youth! Times have changed! Most teenagers now wonder about terrorism ... as well as violence, drugs and guns in their schools.

From kindergarten through college, the specific safety guidance offered students is old worn-out "tips" that continue to avoid the new crime issues of our times. Teenagers *want* and *need* to know what to do with a gun at their head. Unfortunately, updated safety brochures continue to offer only "updated graphics" highlighting the usual safety tips taught by a "cartoon-character crime prevention DOG!" .... AHHHHHH!

> Would we tolerate students learning AIDS prevention from a brochure starring a "cartoon-character AIDS prevention CAT?" Of course not!

Students generally don't like safety talks or traditional safety/ crime prevention programs. Can you guess why? Maybe it's the same reason adults don't them: they feel insulted and talked down to. I know ... because I ASK!

> I listened to a sixth grader recently at an elementary school safety program. She saw the *crime dog puppet* on my demonstration table and asked if I was going to talk about "him." I said: *"No, actually I make fun of him."* She said, *"Good, because when I see that crime dog, I just turn my ears off!"*

TRADITIONAL SAFETY (TIPS) TRAP

How many times have you read or heard (... *or said*) the following:

- ALWAYS know your surroundings
- ONLY park under lights
- DON'T walk alone
- NEVER talk to strangers
- ALWAYS use your COMMON SENSE

Well, brace yourself for the truth! It is ***not possible*** for you to live your life and NEVER walk alone, NEVER talk to strangers, ALWAYS know your surroundings, and ONLY park under street lights, etc. Let me be blunt about something else, preventing and/or surviving crime usually takes **UN**-COMMON SENSE, not common sense! In fact, the choices law-abiding citizens need to survive violent crime are not

"Absolute" rules are impossible to live with!

FASCINATING IDEA:

Let's recycle those traditional crime prevention handouts by giving them to people who NEED behavior restrictions ***... all CRIMINALS leaving jail****. They are the one who should NEVER walk alone, NEVER talk to strangers, ONLY park in well-lit areas, etc. They are the ones who need to use COMMON SENSE to replace their CRIMINAL SENSE!*

"Go ahead and ask me, I know all about judges, lawyers, plea bargaining, probation, legal loopholes ...

Like most law-abidng citizens, you generally respect and follow society's rules. You don't litter, run red lights, make annoying or excessive noises, etc. Yet, there have been many times when you had to put yourself in possible danger or *risk* to fulfill a legitimate *need.* Do you remember feeling scared and hearing the voices of loved ones in your mind WARNING YOU with doubt and guilt: *"You shouldn't be here! You are really asking for it now!"*

Well, that's QUICKSAND! It doesn't matter how big or strong you are. If attacked in that state of mind, you probably will lose because you "internally beat yourself up with guilt ... before a criminal even touches you!"

A quicksand foundation is reality for many people because we are a 24/7 society now. More and more people work long hours, late shifts, attend night-school and travel alone ... thereby surrounding themselves with strangers in darkness. Loved ones forget to compliment the positive results created by all this perseverance and determination. They prefer to sabotage the risk taker's natural strength and courage by the constant warnings of danger.

LEARNED HELPLESSNESS ... A GUILT MACHINE

Years before law-abiding citizens become the victim of a violent crime, many become victims of ***learned helplessness*** and ***assumed vulnerability.*** Decades of conditioning have produced traditional safety wisdom that now has three generations of people believing that their natural strengths and skills are limited, and certainly ***not equal*** to their attacker. This is especially true for women and teenagers. Traditional safety wisdom also implies that *our* behavior contributes significantly to the problem and *we* must adjust *our* lifestyles to "avoid" crime at all times.

If a crime occurs, traditional safety wisdom sometimes appears to imply that our choice put us in a vulnerable position and therefore "**we asked for it....**" by failing to follow those simple *common-sense safety tips.* Some refer to this as *Victim Blaming.*

Traditional safety wisdom ignores the reality that **law-abiding citizens *need* to take risks everyday in order to fulfill their personal and professional responsibilities.**

The price tag of impractical and unreasonable "safety tips" is a toxic poison called **GUILT!** Yes, **GUILT.** No matter what the circumstances are, if you are attacked, others will ***should*** all over you. Why? Because it is what they were *programmed* to do.

I hear the pain of guilt-driven judgment over and over again from heroes (survivors) of crime. Too often, well-meaning people, especially family members, emotionally ***stab*** survivors with negative judgment during a time that they most need loved ones to just LISTEN and give non-verbal, positive support. What instrument is used for the emotional stab? The reminder of those unrealistic "safety tips" of course!

> *Example:*
> A college student is attacked while walking to a night class, after work. She reacts brilliantly, prevents rape, saves her own life, and has her assailant arrested.
>
> Because she is bruised, the police take her to the hospital. Initially, loved ones greet her with hugs and kisses. Words of relief are short lived. By the time she leaves the emergency room, she is ATTACKED AGAIN! This time it is by the loved one(s) who can no longer hold back their programmed judgment:
>
> *"Don't you think you SHOULD have..."* **(STAB)**
> *"Honey, why didn't you...* ***(STAB)***
> *"Haven't I told you many times you should NEVER ...?"* **(STAB)**

OPINIONS

are like noses, everybody has one!

Twenty-five years as a "courage coach" has taught me one absolute reality. When crime survivors seek therapy, it is usually to recover from their hidden pain ... their SECOND attack (STABS) ... the guilt-based judgment, *intended* or *unintended,* from loved ones and friends.

Many survivors cover up their broken heart by saying *"the attack still bothers me."* What they mean is the SECOND (judgment) attack! Loved ones assume they mean the "criminal's attack." In an attempt to offer more comfort, loved ones accidentally give more "judgment commentary" like:

"Well, you've learned a valuable lesson ...
and I'm sure you'll make necessary changes."

Hearing words like that, survivors withdraw further, saying:

"I don't want to talk about it anymore..."

What survivors wish they could say is:

"SHUT UP! I did the best I could!. You weren't there.
It wasn't my fault!
STOP JUDGING ME!"

This misidentification of the real problem (judgment attacks) creates a vicious cycle of miscommunication and unbelievable, long term pain.

When I have the privilege of coaching crime survivors, I always ask, *"Which hurts worse ... pain from the attacker or pain from your loved ones and friends?"* Almost always, their reply is: *"Pain from loved ones and friends."* They are shocked that I know to ask the question.

Some survivors don't even realize that the SECONDARY ATTACK is the source of their un-describable, un-escapable pain ... until I ask the question. Other survivors are so filled with guilt, they actually feel they *deserve* the secondary pain and judgment. Now that is cement shoes on their feet!

GUILT is a huge, truly destructive disease. Unlike a crime which lasts only seconds, minutes or hours, GUILT lasts for weeks, months, years ... and often entire lifetimes! As crime survivors struggle in *quicksand*, they often fight depression while recycling those fresh reminders of common sense "safety tips" (followed perfectly by everyone who has NEVER been attacked...) and they get sadder, madder and sicker every day.

With happiness and trust lost in many areas of their life, crime survivors now feel stupid, scared, helpless, and insulted. A new, sometimes chronic dis-ease is born, called "Fear of Crime." In some cases, "Fear of Crime" grows into "Fear of Everything"...

If not treated effectively, the "Fear of Crime" dis-ease quickly destroys short term and long term goals and dreams. It also destroys friendships, health and happiness. Small pleasures like walking in a park, going on vacation, visiting friends, sitting on a porch, volunteering in the community, etc. seem almost sinful ... because that type of risky behavior could... *invite crime again.*

Our Country's widespread "Fear of Crime" ... is rooted in the poison of **GUILT** and it is absolutely making survivors of crime ... and law-abiding citizens ... **SICK!** In my opinion, the "Fear of Crime" is a much larger problem, than "crime" itself.

IS IT SEXISM, DOUBLE STANDARDS or an ACCIDENT?

With few exceptions, women are "wired to weakness" more severely than men. Their foundations are more likely rooted in quicksand because historically, women are raised with more traditional safety rules and restrictions than men. In fact, what you have read up until now has probably *blown you out of your chair* if you are a woman, and may have *bored you to death* if you are a man.

Look, I am not a feminist or an angry woman. I just report the truth that I see. Guilt driven "safety tips" are programmed LOUDER and MORE CONSISTENTLY in women than men, even in these so called modern and equal times.

Example:

Most parents talk about "safety" very differently to their teenaged daughters than they do their teenaged sons. After 4 to 8 years of high school and/or college, male and female graduates compete for "equal" jobs and "equal" pay that involve "equal risks"... travel, airports, strangers, darkness, parking lots, late working hours, elevators, cab rides, etc.

Who is better prepared to face risk as a successful graduate in the adult work force? Who more likely received the language of confidence and freedom during the formidable, young adult years? Who, at age 22 ... is safer?

Daughters? ... who are usually programmed with language emphasizing limitations and the "fear of everything" because as a young woman:

"You're too trusting!"
"You're too sweet!"
"Look how much smaller you are!"
"I just don't like where you're going."
"Parking lots are DANGEROUS!"
"Girls are just more vulnerable!"
"Someone might take advantage of you!"
"You always think it is going to happen to someone else!"
"You are so naive!"

or

Sons? ...who are programmed with language of freedom and the "assumption" they can handle anything:

"Just do it"
"Just use your head!"
"Get out there!"
"You'll find a way!"
"Hey, No problem. You can handle it!"
"Heads up out there!"
"Make it happen!"
"Take good care of her..."

All this programming *in the name of safety* is so subtle and so damaging. Too often young women start their careers on a foundation rooted in (safety) ***weakness*** which can become career ***"quicksand."*** By contrast, young men have a better chance to start their careers on a foundation rooted in (safety) ***strength*** which leads to career ***"concrete."***

As women try to break the glass ceiling of opportunity in corporate ladder climbing, maybe the problem is not really the "ceiling" but the subtle weakness of their *"quicksand"* foundation.

Example:

A few years ago, I received a call from a lady doctor from a Children's Hospital whose work required her to leave the hospital all hours of the day and night. Responding to my comments on TV about women's careers often rooted in safety "quicksand," she told me (fighting back tears) that her mother was driving her crazy, bragging about "My Daughter the Doctor..." It went something like this:

> *"Oh, I'm so proud of my daughter. But I worry about her so much. You know she's a doctor. She heals children with cancer. She saves lives. But, I HATE IT WHEN SHE WORKS NIGHT SHIFT. One of these days, somebody is going to get her in that parking lot!"*

That's it! QUICKSAND!!! This mom believes her doctor-daughter can save children's lives *on the inside the building,* but she's not capable of saving her own life *outside the building.*

Gently, I asked the doctor: *"Set personal safety aside a minute. What would it mean to your CAREER ... if your mother would say:*

> ***'Oh, I'm so proud of my daughter. She works day and night saving children from cancer. I'll tell you this, only a fool would attack her in the parking lot. She'd WIN! ... because that girl is focused and determined in everything she does.'"***

"Oh, my mom would never say that!" was the doctor's response.

"That's not what I asked," I replied. *"What would it mean to your CAREER if your mom believed in your ability unconditionally?"*

After a long pause, she said: *"It would make a huge difference. Mom obviously believes my strengths are limited to medicine. On a bad day ... sometimes I believe my strengths are limited too. I fight negative self-talk more than I want to admit ... yes, secret self-doubt has held me back in many ways."*

I suggested that the doctor *forgive* her mom. Then I asked her to picture **unrealistic safety rhetoric** as a form of emotional cancer secretly eating away at her career, health, happiness ... and yes, her safety.

I offered this basic advice: *"I know you are busy, but please take a little time to learn our* ***BST*** *message. Then, teach it to your mother for her safety. Be theatrical and make sure she sees, hears, and feels your natural power and confidence. Be realistic. Your mom is from the 'old school' and may be unwilling or unable to change her thinking."*

"Your mom has been programmed to say 'I worry about you.' She believes it is just another way of saying 'I care and I LOVE YOU.' What mom's (and dad's) don't understand is that their adult children interpret 'I worry about you' as '...I don't trust your ability.'"

"This is such a common communication problem in families ... and it is so hurtful. Ultimately, all you can do is CHANGE YOU! Choose to interpret your mom's 'worry' as 'love'... then let it be. Please, do not recycle this toxic safety communication with your children. Help me teach our next generation ***safety willpower and tools****, not excessive worry and rules."*

Family safety is interesting. Have you ever seen weak daughters become weak wives and strong sons become strong husbands? Do most strong husbands you know encourage and support their weak wives to seek personal growth and emotional freedom? Do they support their wife's need to travel for their job, attend night meetings, etc.? Or, are most husbands you know, programmed to innocently enforce **limits and doubts,** like their father did to their mother a generation ago. And why did this happen? ... Fear of Crime!

Dare I suggest that in some families, *intentionally or un-intentionally,* SAFETY is not always about "safety" ... sometimes it grows into "Fear of <u>Change</u>" or C-O-N-T-R-O-L?

In an atmosphere of serious miscommunication and emotional pain, is it possible that in some marriages, constant "safety/control" conflicts lead to serious fighting and divorce? You bet it does!

Example:

A few years ago, I was the opening speaker in the Cleveland Convention Center with thousands of men and women in the audience. At the end of the day, I was buying T-shirts across the street in the "Rock and Roll Hall of Fame" gift shop. A man bumped me reaching for a shirt, and apologized. Then, he recognized me as the morning speaker. He stunned me with his feedback. It went something like this:

"I bought your video tape and called my wife immediately after your presentation this morning. I told her that tomorrow night when I get home, the first thing we are going to do is watch your video together ... because we need to change. Debbie, you have probably saved my marriage."

"Really?" I said. *"What do you mean?"*

"You got through to me. I get it now. My wife has been trying to tell me this stuff for months but her words didn't make sense. She always says 'I am ***smothering*** *her.' She's even threatened to leave me because of it."*

"Wow..." I said. *"You really did listen deeply, didn't you?"* His eyes started to "sweat." (That's a police code-word for cry!)

"Do you see the scar on my face?" he asked. I shook my head "yes." It was huge, from outside his left eye down to the corner of his lip. *"I did that to*

myself in a motorcycle accident when I was 16. Every morning when I shave, I think to myself, ***'If anyone ever scars my beautiful wife like this, I know I will go ballistic!'*** *I just worry so much about her. She is so kind and beautiful ... and naive."*

"How old are you and your wife, and when did you get married?" I asked.

"We are both 30 years old and have been married two years."

"So your naïve wife functioned successfully, on her own, through four years of college and six years as a single attractive woman. And, you fell in love with that strong, independent woman ...right?" I asked.

"Right!" he replied.

"Then you put a wedding ring on her finger, and assumed her strength, independence, personal power and courage went out the church door ... because marriage put you in charge! Now, it's ***your job*** *to protect her! Right?"*

"Oh, you are so right. But it's because I know she doesn't really have any idea of how to protect herself. I thought only I knew what to do. Then this morning, you made me realize that what I knew was pretty weak, especially compared to your ***BST*** *message."*

"So what you are saying is, even though she has NEVER been attacked, your fear for her safety is destroying your marriage, right?" I asked.

"Yes. That's why I can't thank you enough. I believe what you teach. I believe I can do it. What's most important, I believe my wife can do it. It's simple!

We're going to watch the video together and talk. If she feels she can do what you teach, I'm going to back off and stop worrying so much. You made me realize she needs my support, not my rules."

"WOW!" I said as I hugged him. *"This is BIG! I am so happy that our paths crossed and that you had the courage to tell me your story. I believe you speak for more marriages than just your own."*

"I really want to have kids, Debbie, but she keeps saying 'No way would I bring a child into the world with a hyper, over-reactive, worry-wart father like you.' So, if we get like through this ... and have kids, you'll be responsible for that, too. Thanks again."

The convention meeting planners listed our seminar as "Self Defense." For that incredible businessman, it was much, much more.

Do you want more evidence of ***double standards*** in traditional "safety" conditioning?

While visiting the dentist or the doctor, search for and compare the **frequency** and **content** of "self-defense articles and safety tips" in common men's and women's magazines. You'll be fascinated, especially by these two observations I've made:

1. **Self-defense articles are hard to find in common men's magazines.**

   Self–defense "tips" and feature articles appear annually in most women's magazines.

2. **Content comparison (if found) can be comical.** Blatant example: It is common for women to be encouraged NOT to wear neck scarves, string-type jewelry or long strapped purses because of the ease of "strangulation" during an attack. Yet, NEVER have I ever read that men should avoid wearing standard "neckties." Obviously, neckties are tight around the neck and can strangle men easily with one slight tug (... which is why police officers wear "clip-on" ties!)

WHAT CAN YOU DO?

Consider adapting these rarely spoken, fundamental empowerment principles to immediately strengthen your foundation from "quicksand" to "concrete":

You have the RIGHT to go anywhere you NEED to go, 24 hours a day, 7 days a week!

- As a law-abiding, tax-paying adult man or woman of this great Country, you have the technical **RIGHT** to go anywhere you need to go, 24 hours a day, 7 days a week! **(Of course, minors under 18 are subject to family rules and community curfews and restrictions.)**

- FREEDOM does not guarantee that your life will be risk-free! Most of your everyday living will involve low risk choices. Yet someday, a high risk choice may be unavoidable and hopefully survivable. This is life. **NOT ALL CRIMES ARE PREVENTABLE!**

- **Your personal safety is YOUR RESPONSIBILITY ... 100% of the time**. It is your job to at least TRY to save yourself!

  When you choose **high** risk ...
  You are accepting **high** responsibilty.
  RISK and RESPONSIBILTY are partners!

- **Everything you *need* to TRY to save your life ... you already have.**

  That's right ... extraordinary courage, strength, morale backbone, wisdom, power, insight ... it's all in you. Maybe you have not seen it in yourself because there has been too much toxic waste (negative thinking and guilt) covering it up.

  Soon you will learn that if you can reach for a can of soda in your refrigerator, YOU CAN SAVE YOUR LIFE, including weapon attacks!

- **Flush undeserved GUILT.** Choose to release negative conditioning, limiting beliefs, and unrealistic "safety tips" given to you in the past by well-meaning people. Choose to focus on what you CAN do, not what you CAN'T do ... when facing a crisis.

- Restrict the mindless use of ***absolute words*** in *your* everyday language, especially when teaching safety to children. The use of "Don't, Always, Never, etc." in safety education needs to be limited, fair and reasonable. If you say never ... mean NEVER! Example:

  "NEVER talk to strangers" is NOT reasonable.
  "Use caution talking to strangers" is reasonable.

  "Always park under lights" is NOT reasonable.
  "It's a good idea to park under good lighting" is reasonable.

- Gently correct people who carelessly put ***absolute words*** all over you. Example: Response to your parent/spouse if he/she disapproves of your need to walk in parking lots alone:

  > *"I walk with others whenever possible. However, no one has my exact schedule, especially when I work late.* ***I can handle myself.*** *If you really want me to help me be safe, I need your gift of belief in my ability, not your doubt and worry. Your words play in my head when I'm afraid."*
  >
  > *"The next time I am frightened, do you want your words to give me strength ... or ... guilt?"*

- Look over the written safety policy at your school or place of employment. Are ***absolute words*** used fairly? Respectfully ask for an update of old, unrealistic safety tips. Example:

During my first year as a personal safety consultant, a security director from a major corporation called me a week after my seminar with a complaint:

"Gardner, your seminar has just cost this company thousands of dollars!"

"What?" I asked, totally confused.

"Well," he said, "we just threw out 10,000 personal safety booklets which were recently printed for our traveling sales force. Until we heard your message, it never crossed our minds that we were sending our sales reps, alone, all over the world ...with safety information that was in direct conflict with their need to perform their job."

"You know, the traditional stuff ... 'don't walk alone, don't talk to strangers' ...all the things you said that had us laughing in your seminar. So, this morning, we threw them all away. I just thought you'd like to know!"

What delightful feedback! One man listened and created significant change for thousands! His company's safety rhetoric was improved with realistic safety choices adjusted to reflect our **BST** message!

- Accept that everyone needs the same, simple self-defense tools when facing crime, regardless of size, sex, age or physical strength. Effective self-defense needs to be considered a life skill that everyone learns **accurately**, like basic first aid and fire safety.

Now that your emotional foundation is solid **CONCRETE,** my **BST** crime survival message will empower you with crime prevention and survival principles that you can use immediately and remember forever!

Chapter Four

Remember "B"

Mental Righteousness & Self Control

Do you remember the last time you were afraid? Maybe it was a loud noise, a dark parking lot or a late night phone call. Did the *inside* of your body immediately feel different? Did the *outside* of your body struggle to do simple things like:

reach for a light switch?
dial a telephone?
move your legs?
insert a key into a door?
talk ... with volume?
scream for help?

When the fearful event was over, did you tell others,
"...I FROZE?"

- ***No you didn't! Turkeys, chickens, hot dogs and ice cubes freeze!***

What you did was: **HOLD YOUR BREATH!**

- *You were drowning ... without water!*
- *You were sucker-punched ... without a fist!*

Because fear literally **TAKES YOUR BREATH AWAY** ...

- Do something no one can do for you ...

BREATHE!

"B" of **BST** reminds you to **"BREATHE!"**

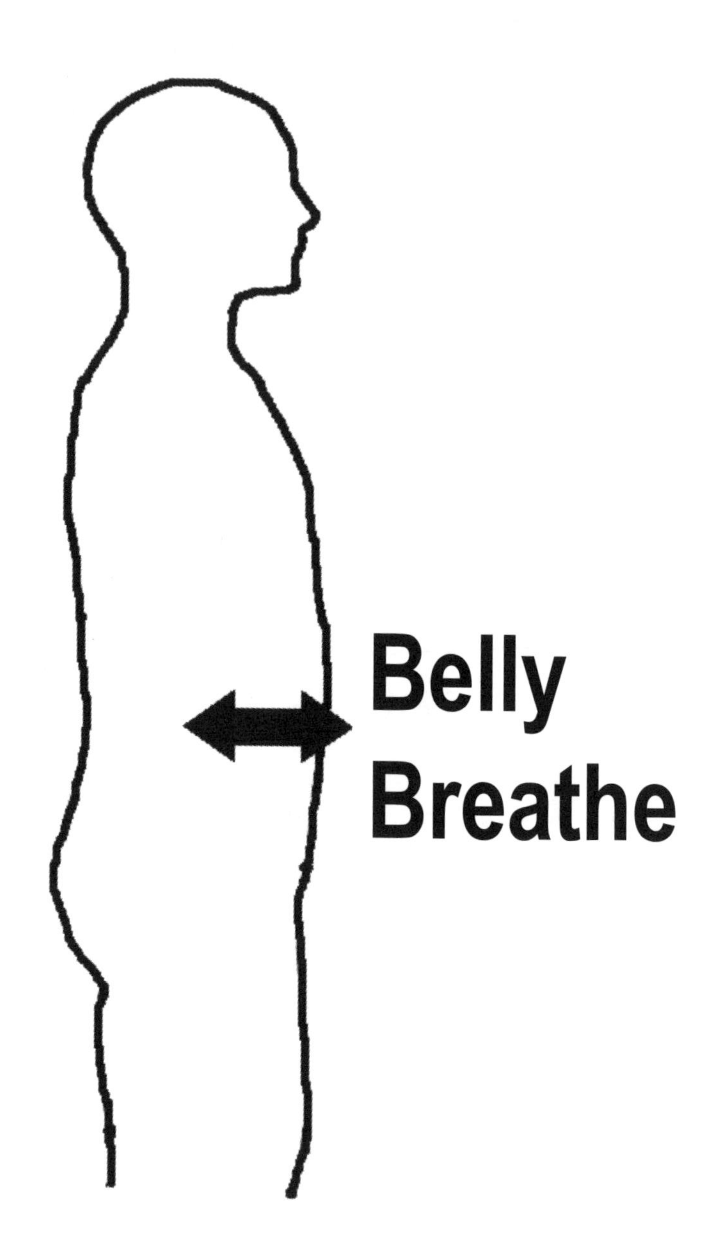
Belly
Breathe

When afraid, BREATHE deeply from your "belly" not from your chest. Think of this deep **"Belly-BREATHING"** as *recovery* or *rescue* breathing. Police and military personnel refer to this as *combat* breathing!

BEWARE! Your first **"Belly-BREATH"** will be very difficult! ***FIGHT FOR IT!!*** Each breath thereafter will be easier. Breathing is a critical life skill. You always need air to live.

Isn't it amazing how "**Belly-BREATHING"** is emphasized in singing, sports, public speaking, childbirth and exercise classes ... but is not mentioned in crime prevention and safety brochures?

GET A "GRIP!"

Do you remember feeling your HEART beat wildly the last time you were afraid?

Medical explanations for fear induced chemical and circulation changes in your blood are very complicated. To keep things simple, let's just agree that your heart beats *faster* and feels *larger* than normal when you are afraid. This change is real and often referred to as the body's preparation for the FIGHT, FREEZE OR FLIGHT SYNDROME.

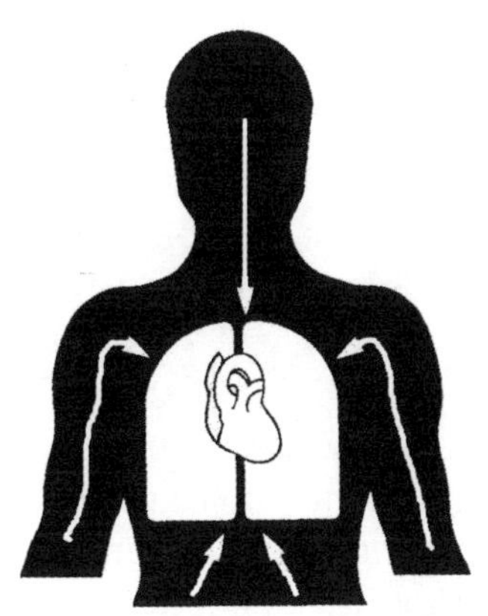

Fight, Freeze or Flight Syndrome

Visualize your overworked, enlarged heart **SUCKING** blood from your extremities, specifically your head, hands and feet.

This rapid change from *normal* to *accelerated* blood flow ... from your extremities to your heart, explains why your head, hands and feet do not seem to work properly when you are afraid.

After a crisis, have you ever heard people say:

"I just couldn't move!"
"My mind went blank!"
"Her face was as white as a ghost!"
"My key wouldn't go in the lock!"
"He kept misdialing 9-1-1"
"My legs wouldn't move!"
"I was moving in slow motion!"
"I was paralyzed!"
"My body felt like lead!"

Listen to these crisis survivors! They are reporting the truth! They are not exaggerating or making up excuses. These words graphically describe the physiological consequences that occur when chemical changes (i.e., adrenalin, etc.) mix with the shifting flow of oxygenated blood.

"The RUSH" vs. "The CREEPS"

Isn't it interesting how your BRAIN interprets **FEAR** as "*good*" or "*bad*" ... because physiologically, your body reacts exactly the same!

In a ***positive*** fearful experience, we call the feeling a high or a ***RUSH.*** Examples: winning a BIG lottery, riding a roller coaster, competitive sports accomplishments, bungee jumping, etc.

> In a ***negative*** fearful experience, we call the feeling "the ***CREEPS***" (which accurately describe sensations of heaviness when oxygenated blood "creeps" from the extremities towards the heart!) Examples: scary noises, dark parking lots, frightening movies, etc.

To regain proper control of your blood flow, you need to:

Grip your hands (*open* and *close)* to force your enlarged heart to send that high-octane *adrenaline-filled* oxygenated blood back to your extremities.

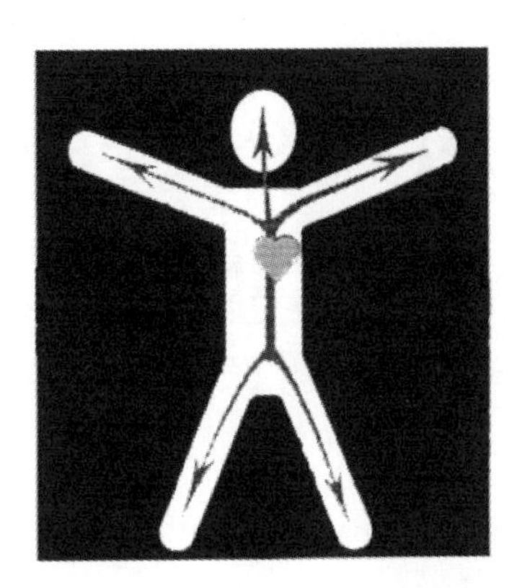

Your heart muscle is amazing. It is a basic magical "pump." The deliberate action of GRIPPING your fists will automatically circulate blood back to your arms, legs, hands and feet.

Deep "Belly-**BREATHING**" and repeated "Hand-**GRIPPING**" are the key to enhancing your body's ability for *peak performance,* in any crisis, especially *crime survival.*

CRIME vs. CARS

Statistics consistently report that law-abiding citizens are more likely to be injured or killed in a car crash than a violent crime. Yet, we tend to ignore *driving hazards* and devote most of our **fear energy** to *crime hazards.*

If you drive, odds are you have already saved your life (and others) many times. When threatened, **you didn't FREEZE!** You made immediate, accurate choices and movements that saved your life. You did this **without** the benefit of repetitious physical defensive driving classes. You just did it!

How specifically did you save yourself?

Well, what were your hand(s) doing?

GRIPPING ... the steering wheel!

Normal Driving

In a defensive driving maneuver, GRIPPING keeps you ready ... without thinking about being ready.

1. Your *head* makes correct, rapid decisions
2. Your *hand(s)* turn the steering wheel
3. Your *foot* switches from the gas pedal to the brake rapidly!

This all happens in a split second! Amazing!

Now think about "crisis driving" ... those times you choose to continue to drive in fog, ice, snow, rain, thunderstorms, etc. Without thinking about it, you *naturally* activate the three critical actions needed for ***life-saving peak performance:***

Crisis Driving

1. **You Belly-BREATHE!**
   ... so deeply, your windshield is about to blow off your car!

2. **You "double" GRIP!**
   ...BOTH hands on the steering wheel because one grip is not enough!

3. **You focus on POSITIVE THOUGHTS!**
   "O.K. I can do this! Yes I can! OK. OK! I'm OK right now! I can do this!"

   I bet you have even *positively lied to yourself* for a safe driving outcome! C'mon! You didn't feel **... *"OK"* ...** driving in a thick fog. You were ***terrified!***

Drivers! Be excited! You have a proven record of success for preventing crisis and physically saving your life ... in a car. Believe that you **can** and **will** duplicate that success ... in a test with violence!

The Power of LOVE

If positive thoughts represent the third action needed for peak performance and self-control, are you wondering what specific thoughts are **BST** for crime survival?

Before I make a suggestion, I'm wondering if you have ever had this (negative) thought ...

If I'm attacked, I don't know what I will do ...
I'll probably FREEZE!

If you are like most people I've tested, your answer is: *"YES!"*

OK! This time think about someone you LOVE! Visualize walking with an older, weaker, friend or loved one *(your mom, dad, sister, brother, grandmother, grandfather, etc.)* when all of a sudden a violent person rushes past you and goes directly at your _______ (Mother!) Is this your immediate reaction ... ?

"You try to touch my ________ (mother) violently ... I will knock you across the street ... "

Whoa! Where did that positive attitude come from?

This time, visualize walking with a smaller, weaker friend or loved-one (your child, grandchild, baby-sister, baby-brother, niece, nephew, etc.) when all of a sudden a violent person rushes past you and goes directly after your _____ (Child!) Is your immediate reaction ...

"You try to attack my _____ (child) violently ... I'll KILL you!"

Whoa! KILL? ... What a powerful yet frightening four-letter word! Where did that attitude come from?

When focusing on saving the life of a LOVED ONE:

- ☺ Why is your attitude and self-talk naturally strong?
- ☺ Why are you confident that you won't … FREEZE?
- ☺ Why do you blindly believe you can do anything?
- ☺ Why don't you need pepper spray, stun guns, sound alarms, police or security?
- ☺ Why are you fearless of the consequences … police reports, lawsuits, trials and if all goes wrong … "jail time?"
- ☺ Why are you comfortable assuming you'll "find a way" … or die TRYING?

ANSWER: ***Because when your HEART focuses on saving a LOVED ONE … <u>WINNING</u> is the only acceptable outcome!***

The BST positive thoughts … are thoughts of

LOVED ONES!

CRITICAL QUESTION: Why then, does the thought of "saving *yourself*" create such **doubt** and **fear?**

ANSWER: ***Because your name is not on your …"LOVED ONES" List!***

MY 'LOVED ONES' LIST ***"I can do anything for..."***
1. **ME**
2.
3.
4.
5.
6.
7.
8.
9.

That's right! You have given yourself permission to save everyone you love ... but **YOU!** As your Courage Coach, I encourage you to make immediate attitude adjustments NOW!

♥ **Put your name at the top of your "LOVED ONES" List!**

Yes, the TOP! Surviving a crime requires you to be selfish and self-centered. **"Me FIRST"** is a great crime survival plan because

"LOVE is POWER!"

Adjust your attitude to believe you can *naturally do* for you, what you already know and believe you can do for your *loved ones.*

HOMEWORK: Listen to the words of the song "Greatest Love of All" by Whitney Houston ...

♫ ***"Learning to LOVE YOURSELF ... is the Greatest Love of All ..."*** ♫

♥ **Accept that a direct crime against you is also a DIRECT CRIME against your loved ones!**

Ask crime survivors... they will tell you that loved ones are directly attacked too, emotionally. Emotional injury to your loved ones, through YOUR SKIN, is not acceptable. Let the thought of loved ones injured, ***physically or emotionally,*** makes your blood naturally boil!

Sometimes, loved ones' devastation is actually worse than survivors' because loved ones allow their mind to exaggerate the facts. Some loved ones, vocally or silently, actually share blame for the crime's occurrence. Parents ... especially dads and husbands, often feel they failed in their role as "Family Protector" when a crime occurs.

Nagging Protectors' Guilt is why some crime survivors are plagued with excessive judgment language from the family protector:

*"**YOU** should not have been there..."*

When what they are saying to themselves is,

"I should not have let you be there..."

- ***NEVER be afraid ... to be afraid! FEAR is GOOD ... when you learn to control it!***

Fear causes changes inside your body that shuts you down or turns you on! **Self-control in a crisis is your choice:**

... You can do nothing
or
... You can courageously **BREATHE! GRIP!** And visualize **LOVED ONES!**

When self-control is activated your heart releases **LOVE FIRE!** *It melts your "freeze" and transforms you with miraculous "energy", immeasurable "strength" and abundant "courage" to do what's right.*

For Love, I can do anything!

Holding Breath
Negative Self-Talk

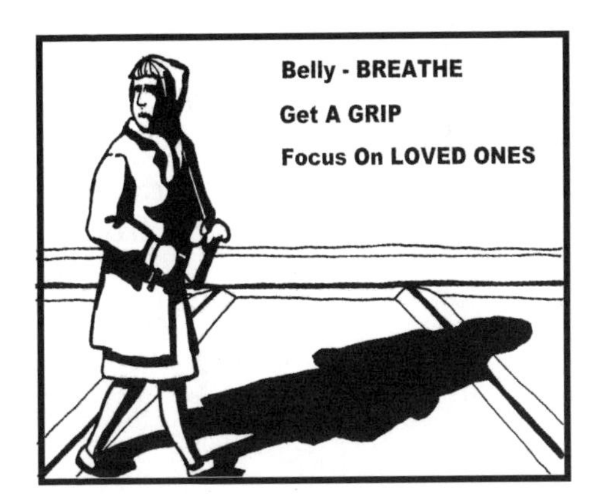
Belly - BREATHE
Get A GRIP
Focus On LOVED ONES

♥ **LOOK Around! Show EYE-FIRE from your heart!**

It is impossible to control what you are not willing to see. When you feel the ***creeps***, rapidly rotate your head from side to side. Whether you see someone or not, expose your heart's attitude by speaking *non-verbally* ... through the intensity of your **EYE-FIRE:**

"Keep off my _________" (child, parent, spouse, etc).

Pretend your loved one(s) are right there with you!

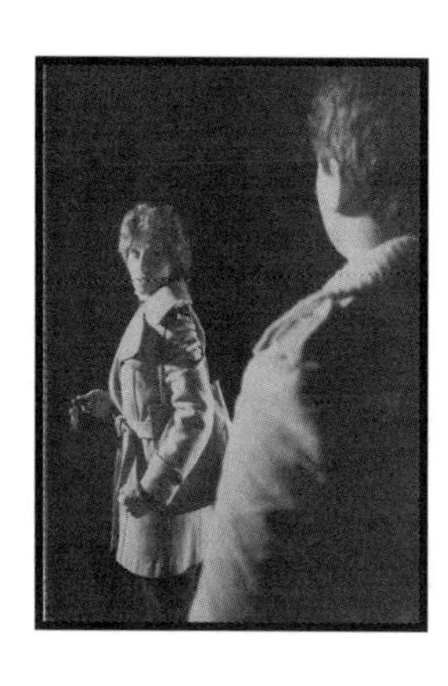

Eye contact directed towards a possible threat does not need to be a "stare down" but rather constant monitoring that lets a possible threat know, *"I'm watching you ... and I am in control of ME!"*

You will never be able to prove that you prevented crimes by "turning on" your **EYE-FIRE!** Unfortunately, it is impossible to prove what doesn't occur. Please do not let the lack of proof stop you from celebrating your success!

When your courage is tested and you win, you build upon an even higher degree of self-love and trust.

Watch professional and Olympic athletes carefully. They are masters at demonstrating self-control and **peak performance** because they are in crisis at every competition. If they do not consistently succeed, they lose status and millions of dollars. Truly great athletes in any sport, *consciously* or *unconsciously* ... **Belly-BREATHE, GRIP,** and **positively FOCUS** on achieving their goal.

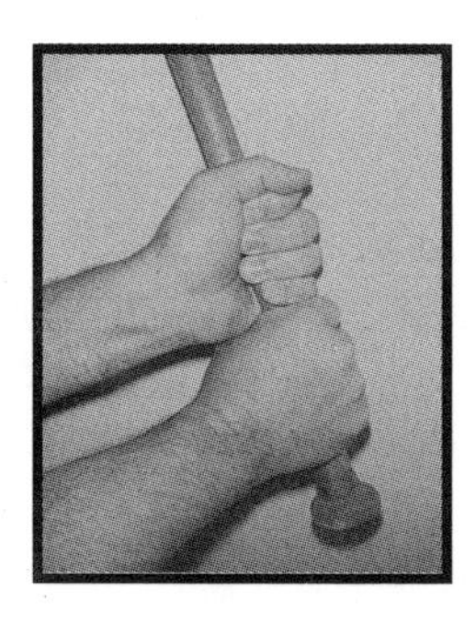

Do you think baseball and golf are boring to watch on TV? That's because most of the action is a "MIND GAME" filled with ... BREATHING and GRIPPING ... not touching the ball!

A wonderful example of a truly great athlete who masters self-control is Tiger Woods. When under pressure at a golf tournament, he grabs his golf club, walks slowly and takes extra time to **"Belly-BREATHE!"** He adjusts his **GRIP** multiple times. Practice swings and shifting his weight from leg to leg are additional ways he circulates blood until he *feels right* positioning his feet into the ground. His focus is intense and you can be sure his ***self-talk*** **is POSITIVE** as he prepares to swing. He then **visualizes** where he wants the ball to go before he ever touches it.

In a magazine article featuring Tiger Wood's domination in professional golf, hockey-legend Wayne Gretzky commented:

"Most golfers can't believe they won. Tiger sounds like he expected to win ... or can't believe he didn't!" [1]

Wouldn't you love to know *exactly* what Tiger says to himself preparing for critical shots? You can be sure thoughts like: "Gee, this is tough! I ***shouldn't*** be here today..." are not in Tiger's mind. Those thoughts are in the minds of losers!

[1] Time Magazine, September 2001

Peak performance in any crisis, especially crime survival, requires self-talk that unites the conscious and subconscious minds with words that are:

- **Passionate ...** reflecting ***intense*** *emotions*
- **Positive ... *"I can do this"***
  ... NOT "I can't, shouldn't" etc.
- **Present Tense ... *"RIGHT NOW* ...** I'm OK!"

If athletes have a bad day, TV commentators say things like:

*"He's lost his **focus**!*
OR
*She sure is in a **slump!**"*

These cliché's reflect the loss of an athlete's *inner* mind-game, NOT an athlete's loss of physical skills or strengths. You do not need to be a professional athlete to believe:

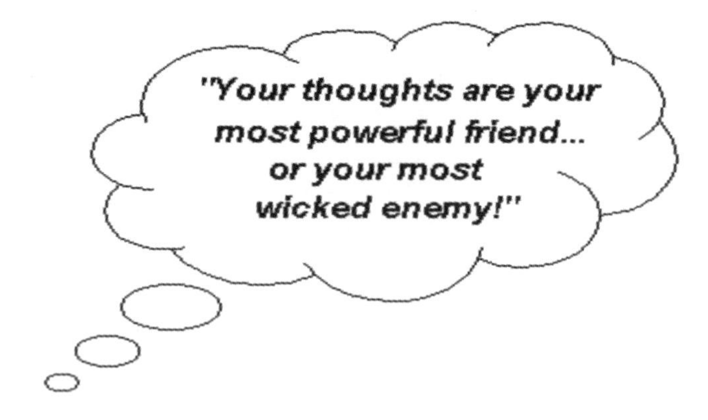

SUMMARY of REMEMBER "B"

Remember that **"B"** of **BST** summarizes **SELF-CONTROL**...

BREATHE! ... to control ***oxygen***

- **GRIP** ... to control ***blood***
- **LOVE** ... to control ***positive thoughts***

With "inside" control accomplished, focus on the "outside" ...

- **LOOK!** ... with **EYE-FIRE!**

"*Feeling* in control" on the *inside* of your body while ...
"*Looking* in control" on the *outside* of your body ...
will STOP many crimes before they start!

YOU JUST CAN'T PROVE IT!

On rare occasions, a *threat* may not go away. In that case you need to escalate to **"S"** ... and then possibly **"T"** ... of the **BST** ***Crime Survival*** message in order to save your life!

"If you face just one opponent ...
And doubt yourself ...
You are already OUTNUMBERED!"

Dan Millman

BONUS APPLICATIONS!

We all experience fear many places besides crime survival. The **BST Mental** actions for self-control can be applied other places too!

In addition to **Belly-BREATHING** and **thinking POSITIVE** ... get a **GRIP** in these unique ways:

Under stress?	Grip a "stress ball"
Verbal conflict at work?	Grip a "glue stick" as you talk
Nervous about a speech?	Grip a "pointer" or "dry erase marker"
Important test at school?	Grip a "magic marker" in non-writing hand
Scared walking?	Grip a "handle" on your keys, or cell phone, pager, water bottle, purse strap
Medical/dental fear?	Grip "arms of a chair," "rolled up magazine" and "cross your legs at your ankles"
Baby crying?	Give something to GRIP ... blanket, bottle, pacifier, toy, etc. **(OOPS, you already know that one!)**
Need improved sports performance?	GRIP more until you "feel right"

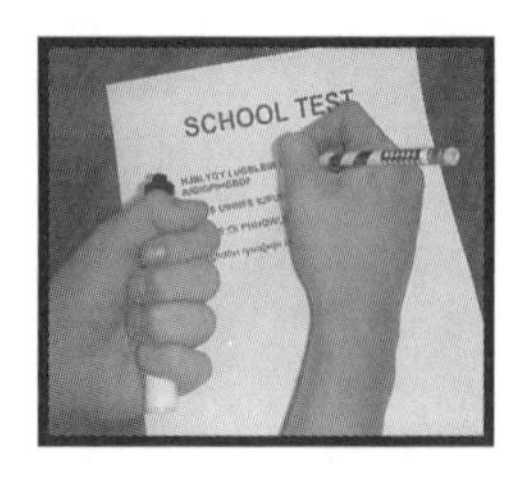

Nothing available to grip? Then squeeze your hands, like you do when your hands are cold.

JUST REMAIN "CALM" ... makes people furious!

Have you ever made some one even *madder* by telling them to *calm down*? Have you ever read emergency procedures that suggest *remain calm?*

PLEASE STOP using and accepting those meaningless phrases! They are "hollow" ... and offer **no** specific actions to help a person who is mad, upset or in crisis! Help someone by giving specific action ideas like:

- **Belly-BREATHE**
- **GRIP you hands**
- **THINK of "____________________"**

(offer a *positive thought* to change their focus.)

My Goal: Meaningful safety billboards like this ...
all over the country!

SUCCESS STORIES!

<u>GRIPPER!</u>

A woman called me for *courage coaching* many times because of her tremendous fear of her ex-husband. She had him arrested for very serious federal crimes. While he was in jail, he hired a "hit man" to kill her and her son. The "hit man" missed.

Because of her amazing courage and self-control, (**breathing, gripping** and concentrating on **protecting her son**) she was able to give the police a description of her attacker. The police were then able to arrest the "hit man" too. She eventually testified brilliantly against both in federal court.

When the trial was over, she sent me a beautiful thank you note. She mentioned the difficulties about the trial and stated that she GRIPPED a tube of "ChapStick"™ during her entire two-hour testimony. Her self-control led to a conviction and 44 years in prison for both her "ex" and the "hit-man!"

"What a courageous hero!"

Debbie —
Thanks so much for your note. I really appreciated you thinking of me. The trial is over and thank the Lord for a guilty verdict! It was extremely stressful, but I have you know that I kept my Chap stick in hand -- gripping & un-gripping -- while on the stand for over two hours. I learned from an expert!! Hopefully the oxygen got to brain and I answered all questions well. Sentencing is April 21st & May 11th — please keep us in your prayers!

LOVERS!

Mike and I teach police officers to keep their loved ones "on duty" with them by attaching a photo of their family on the cruiser's dashboard.

When responding to a dangerous situation, officers are encouraged to **Belly-BREATHE**, and intensely **GRIP** their steering wheel as they park their cruiser (deliberating fueling oxygenated blood to their extremities ... just like millionaire athletes in crisis) ... and **LOOK** at their family for immediate, positive empowerment.

One of Mike's fellow officers so believes in this concept that he took it a step further. In addition to putting a picture of his family on his dashboard, he put an **8"x 10" enlarged photo of his infant in his police hat** for "close" added inspiration!

Peace is not the "absence of conflict",
but the ability to COPE with it.

Chapter Five

Remember "S"

Take Control Verbally

Wouldn't it be great if your "self control" and "eye-fire" could stop all criminals? Unfortunately, in some attacks, taking control **MENTALLY** is just the foundation. You may need to escalate by taking control **VERBALLY.**

Verbal power is the tool you need to keep people you are not sure of out of your personal space. I'm sure you know you have the *right* to protect your *body* at all times, but did you know that you also have the *right* to defend your *personal space?* In most cases, attackers need to close in on their victims' **personal space** in order to rob, rape, mug, or murder.

"S" of BST reminds you to:

Protect Your...

SPACE!

Visualize your *normal personal space* as a hula-hoop around your body.

Without thinking about it, courteous people keep natural, comfortable *elbow-room* distance from one another.

The range of your personal **space** may change many times during the day. Sometimes you voluntarily give up your **space** like on crowded elevators or at crowded sporting events.

Example: At the end of the day, a businesswoman voluntarily gives up her space when she steps into a crowded elevator. Walking off the elevator into the lobby, her space expands immediately to *elbow room.* In the parking lot, her personal space expands to the *width of many cars.* If she works overtime and hers is the only car in the company's private parking lot, technically ... the *entire parking lot* is her personal space because she is the only person who belongs there!

Your body warns you when your **space** is "being invaded!" Your breathing accelerates and your heart beats faster. As danger approaches, people often say they ***feel the CREEPS.*** Remember, that is a literal explanation of what is actually happening *inside* a fear-filled body! When danger arises, your normal flow of blood and oxygen changes ... it ***CREEPS*** rapidly towards the center of your body to WARN YOU that something is wrong ... probably something you can't even see!

LISTEN TO YOUR BODY! Your *body* doesn't lie! Sadly, your *brain* will not make *logical sense* of your fear ... until later!

> In his best selling book The Gift of Fear, author Gavin de Becker pleads with his readers to trust their "intuition" as a life-skill for preventing violence. He explains:
>
> "Intuition ... is knowing without knowing **why**!"

CHANGE COLORS

Do you think of yourself as a **GOLDEN Person** ... a person who lives by the *GOLDEN RULE ... "Do unto others as you would have them do unto you?"* In other words, are you nice? Do you care, give, help, share, and donate ... regularly?

THANK YOU! People like you make this Country great!

Stop believing that because you are GOLDEN ... you are *weak!* **YOU ARE NOT WEAK**! If anything, you are only **STUCK**! Specifically, you are *uncomfortable, untrained* or *too afraid* to escalate from the kindness of GOLD to the needed confrontational behavior of ORANGE ... or even RED choices.

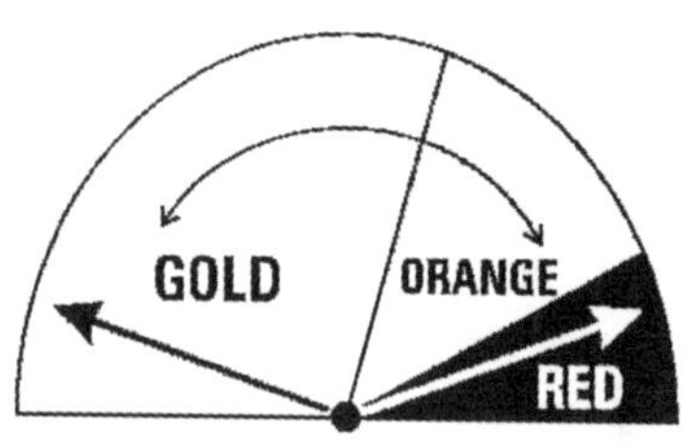

Think of this color change as ACTING! Actors set aside their true personality in order to *say or do* whatever it takes to create their character. You may need to *say or do* whatever it takes ... to save your life!

You are somewhat familiar with "acting out" temperament change! Your life is not perfect! Admit it! You have already experienced **ORANGE,** the color of ***frustration***... many times. Remember the last time you were upset when you:

Ran out of gas?
Argued with a friend?
Locked your keys in the car?

You weren't "nice" (GOLDEN) ... you were "mad" (ORANGE)!

What color are the construction barrels on the highway when you are stuck in traffic? ORANGE! They could be bright green or yellow. No, they are frustrating! They are ORANGE! Admit it, they cause you to ***feel*** ORANGE and ***talk*** ORANGE!

When you are ORANGE, you tend to raise your volume and verbally "bark" at people. You use degrees of ORANGE temperament ... from ***goldish-orange*** (returning cold french fries at a fast food restaurant) to ***reddish-orange*** (screaming at a reckless driver for almost running over a family member.) Your verbal response is an attempt to correct a "wrong" done against you.

RED is the color of **rage**! **RED** is a condition that scares and appalls GOLDEN people like you because it is so opposite of who you are. Unfortunately, RED personalities exist in our society.

Except for severe cases of mental illness, the cause of RED behavior is usually rooted in excessive intoxication from **DRUGS, ALCOHOL** and/or **HATRED!** This intoxication causes RED criminals to be **emotionally, morally** and **physically numb** at the time they attack.

DRUGS! ALCOHOL! HATRED!

No Conscience
Extreme Strength
Feels NO Pain

Effective crime prevention and survival requires you to match the color of your attacker, ***verbally*** first... then ***physically***.

It is important for you to know:

WHO criminals are ...
WHAT they want ...
HOW they get into your personal space ...

<u>WHO</u> ATTACKS? <u>WHAT</u> DO THEY WANT?

Let's keep it simple. FOUR types of criminals want up to THREE things in a violent attack:

1. THIEVES

... want your PROPERTY!

There are several specific titles for thieves: bank robbers, carjackers, purse-snatchers, house-burglars, shoplifters, con-men, etc. Usually, thieves prefer to work *behind* your back because they are less likely to be seen and arrested. **Thieves who are bold enough to steal directly from you can become very dangerous during an attack!**

Remember, thieves specifically want ... **MONEY!** They will take anything in addition to cash, like your purse, briefcase, wallet, credit cards, jewelry, silver, guns, stereo, TV, car, etc. Thieves usually sell what they steal ... for CASH to support their lifestyle, as well as expensive habits like *drug abuse, drug trafficking, alcohol abuse, gambling addictions and/or gambling debt.*

Thieves, usually don't want to hurt *you* ... they just want your *stuff* which is why police consistently encourage citizens not to resist or *physically* fight thieves. I agree, and will explain this in more detail later.

What are your odds of *physically* surviving a **THIEF**? ANSWER: ***Very Good!***

You will need to use **M**ental and **V**erbal choices. If a thief gets **mad** (because of severe intoxication ... or maybe you didn't have what he wanted...or you didn't comply fast enough) **your choices may need to escalate to physical.**

(Remember: **MVp**)

MY PET PEEVE WITH THIEVES! *As a law abiding, tax-paying citizen, THIEVES make me mad not only because they traumatize people when they steal but because, they DON'T PAY TAXES on their income! To me, every theft is a* ***double crime*** *against society.*

Think about how rich you would be if you did not pay taxes on your daily income! When a thief gets $100 for selling stolen prescription pills, he keeps $100. If you work all day and legally make $100, your actual take-home pay is what? $70? $65?

Why aren't serious thieves and drug dealers regularly charged with "tax evasion" by the IRS? *Think about the BILLIONS of dollars that could be generated to improve schools, roads, etc. The bonus of extra federal prison time for tax envasion might* ***STOP*** *at least a few thieves from believing that: "CRIME PAYS..." because right now ... it does! Consequences for most levels of "theft" are ridiculous. Law abiding citizens deserve better.*

2. FRUSTRATED criminals
... want to *hurt* your BODY!

An enormous amount of crimes are committed by people who are emotionally *hurting* and *just can't take it anymore!* The source of their *hurting* varies from:

UNDESERVED MISFORTUNES *outside* of their control, i.e.,

Severe physical illness
Severe mental illness
Depression
Family death
Family problems
Homelessness
Sexual assault
Physical assault
Unemployment
Troubled childhood
Workplace problems

... to **BAD CHOICES** *within* their control, i.e.,

Alcohol abuse
Drug abuse
Pornography
Selfishness
Gambling
Illiteracy
Anger
Revenge
Jealousy
Laziness
Loneliness

These and other sources of ***hurt*** may serve as reasons to help us understand a criminal's behavior, but they should NEVER be tolerated as **acceptable excuses** for causing crime.

The crimes **frustrated** people commit cause pain from the victim's head to their toes. Examples:

Hang up phone calls	Death threats
Physical assault	Abduction
Sexual assault	Child abuse
Domestic violence	Bullying
Workplace violence	Torture
School violence	Animal abuse

A ***frustrated*** criminal's goal is not necessarily that you die but that you ***suffer!*** Simply stated:

"HURT" people ... *HURT* people!

> What are the odds of *physically* surviving a **FRUSTRATED** criminal? Answer: ***GOOD!***
>
> **Guessing the behavior of people whose "hearts are broken" can be very difficult.** (Frustrated workers *sometimes* kill co-workers, frustrated wives *sometimes* kill husbands, etc.) You will need **Mental** and **Verbal** choices ...and if desperate, **Physical** choices.
>
> **(**Remember**: MVP)**

3. PSYCHOTIC criminals
... want your LIFE!

When ***enraged psychopath or sociopath*** criminals attack, they are physically, morally and emotionally *numb and out of control!* They do not listen, so talk downs and negotiations are usually impossible.

Criminals in a ***psychotic rage*** are not interested in money or just hurting you ... they want you to die! Many times, they then kill themselves. Examples of these crimes are:

- Murder
- Mass Murder
- Suicide-by-Police
- Murder/Suicide
- Serial Murder

What are the odds of *physically* surviving a **PSYCHOTIC** criminal? ANSWER: **POOR!**

A PSYCHOTIC criminal "*takes your breath away*" and attacks rapidly. You will have very little time to activate m̲ental or v̲erbal choices ...you will need a rapid, accurate **P̲HYSICAL** strike.

(Remember: **mvP̲**)

4. ASSASSIN/HIT-MAN
... wants your LIFE!

This type of criminal is prepared. He attacks from a distance and uses dangerous weapons (high powered guns/ rifles, bombs, poison, etc.)

Good News: most street criminals do not attack like this.

Bad News: this type of crime is increasing in our Country and worldwide, especially in the illegal drug industry.

Stop assuming assassinations only happen to presidents and other heads of state. Drug traffickers and even spouses are ordering "hits for hire" in growing numbers! Examples of these types of crimes:

Murder for hire	Home invasions
Drive by shooting	Political "hits"
Police-targeted ambush	Workplace shootings
School shootings	Suicide bombers

Here is a hard question. Which category of criminal behavior would you use to describe a **TERRORIST** or **GANG** member?

They **STEAL**	*(identities, weapons, money in order to advance their cause, ideology and/or religion.)*
They **HURT**	*("terrorize" by threats, assaults, abductions, rape, etc.)*
They **KILL**	*(close range ... and at a distance.)*

TERRORISTS and **GANG** members fit **ALL** criminal categories which is why they are so frightening!

I believe free societies need to give serious and adequate consequences to "thieves" ... because we have no idea who they *really* are and what they *really* want. "Theft" is NOT minor crime!

> *The September 11th, 2001 terrorist tragedy taught lessons on the serious consequences of simple identity theft and fraud from U.S. vehicle license bureaus! Terrorists used fake I.D.'s as the foundation of their master plan.*

What are the odds of *physically* surviving an **ASSASSIN**? ANSWER: **Extremely POOR!**

If fate allows you to survive an assassins' "hit" you will need a rapid, accurate ***PHYSICAL*** strike ... if you are close enough!

(Remember: **mvP**)

IN SUMMARY ...

WHO ARE THEY?
THIEF
FRUSTRATED
PSYCHOTIC
ASSASSIN
WHAT DO THEY WANT?
MY PROPERTY
MY BODY
(Assault/Hostage/Rape)
MY LIFE

HOW DO CRIMINALS GET INTO YOUR SPACE?

Except for the rare distance-attack by an assassin, most criminals attack by getting close and invading your **personal space** one of three ways:

1. CONVERSATION Attack

A criminal approaches you casually and starts a ***conversation*** ...usually by asking a simple question like:

"What time is it ...?"
"Do you know where ...?
"Do you have change for ...?

Criminals assume that you and other GOLDEN people are likely to:

- Allow your **MIND** to be "distracted" ... thinking about the answer to the question
- Allow your **HANDS** to be "tied up" ... touching your watch, "pointing out" directions or digging in your pocket/purse for items
- Allow your **EYES** to "look away" ... following your hands

While you are attempting to "help", a criminal will attack the immediate second you **look away**.

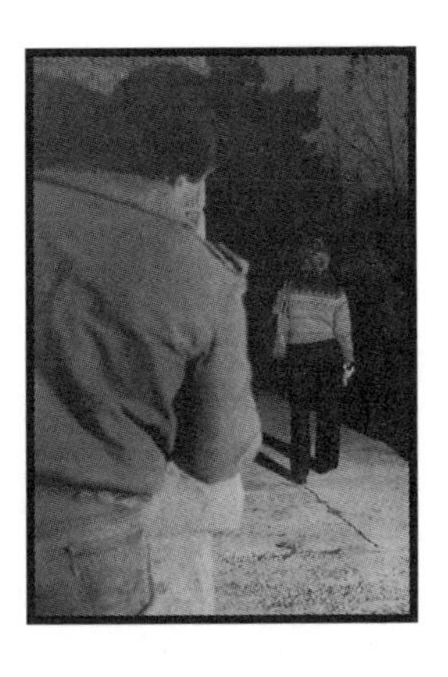

2. FOLLOWING Attack

You feel someone walking near you, getting **abnormally** close at a fast pace. In this style of attack, criminals know you and other GOLDEN people are likely to telegraph your fear by:

- Locking your **EYES** forward in tunnel-vision
- **STIFFENING** body movements
- **BEATING YOURSELF UP** on the inside
  ... with negative thoughts and self-talk
  (By the time he attacks, you're already weak!)

In a "following" attack, criminals watch your fear-filled, **non-response** to their stalking presence ... then charge rapidly at you ... usually from behind.

3. SURPRISE Attack

You see nothing. You hear nothing. You feel no danger. There is no warning. Criminals know you and other GOLDEN people are likely to:

- **STOP BREATHING**
- **MELT** to the ground

When criminals attack by **surprise,** they assume they'll gain complete control immediately.

LEARN TO DEFEND YOUR SPACE

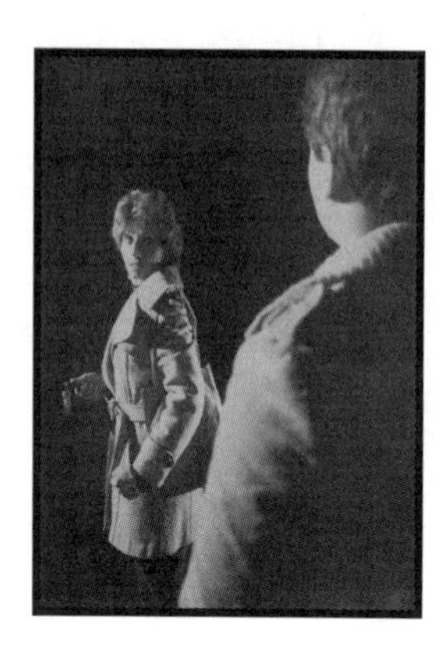

Preventing a ...
CONVERSATION Attack

Strangers talk to strangers all the time. C'mon! We need each other! Feel good knowing most strangers are GOLDEN people and do not intend to attack you when they talk or ask for help.

Your challenge is to identify, then act differently (ORANGE or RED) towards that **ONE**–in-a-million stranger who is trying to set you up.

PAY ATTENTION TO YOUR BODY'S NATURAL WARNING SYSTEM! Let the feeling of oxygen and blood ***creeping*** rapidly to the center of your body ... be your guide!

When a stranger walks towards you, creating the feeling of the **CREEPS** ... and begins to talk or ask questions:

- ☑ **BREATHE**, Grip and Visualize LOVED ONES!
- ☑ Make direct **EYE** contact and hold it!
- ☑ **STEP BACK** to reclaim your **SPACE** (re-draw an invisible hula-hoop line)
- ☑ Give a confident, **NEGATIVE RESPONSE** to questions or comments, like:

"... I don't have the time"
"... I don't know the directions"
"... I don't have any change"

You are **ALLOWED to LIE**! ... NOT help! NOT give! NOT share! NOT care! NOT be GOLDEN!

What's likely to happen:

- **If the stranger is a "decent" person ...**
  simply wanting the answer to a question, he will just GO AWAY... and ask someone else. His day is not ruined! He moves on. You are safe.

  Do not feel bad that you misjudged him and did not help! **Who you helped ... was YOU** and your loved ones! You listened to your body's warning alarm and put your need to be safe ... first! Congratulations!

- **If the stranger is a "potential criminal" ... he will:**

  - **IGNORE** your negative response
  - **STEP FORWARD** into your **SPACE**
  - **ASK** another question or keep talking

YOU ARE IN TROUBLE!

Nice people *won't* do that! Turn **ORANGE** as you:

☑ **Belly-BREATHE** again
☑ Keep **CONSTANT EYE** contact
☑ **STEP BACK** to reclaim your space AGAIN
☑ **POINT your finger** (like a gun) to show your
... ORANGE attitude
... new SPACE (hula-hoop) LINE!
☑ **Say "NO"** (negative response) **LOUDLY**
to all questions and comments

Repeat. Verbally, go from ORANGE to RED if needed!

Obviously, if you can **RUN** ... get out of there! Odds are however, you are trapped up against a parked car, building or some physical barrier. This is not your fault. Criminals set-up *fake* conversation to create traps.

One of two responses are likely to happen when you turn

ORANGISH/RED

- **He will go away ...** because you are too difficult to trick. He is looking for a "victim" not a "hassle." He walks away, looking for a new victim. ***You WON! You just can't prove it!***

OR

- **He attacks ...** by stepping rapidly into your space. He grabs or demands your property ...

  - ☑ **BREATHE!**
  - ☑ **GIVE UP YOUR PROPERTY** ***fast***
  - ☑ **LOOK at him** to create a "mental photograph"
  - ☑ **Give 9-1-1 a description**
  - ☑ **CELEBRATE!** (See Chapter 7)

... OH, NO! He didn't go away!

Be careful if a criminal takes your property and STOPS! He's ANGRY! You don't have "enough" of what he wants. If he throws your property to the ground and *comes rapidly towards you AGAIN ...*

THIS CRIMINAL IS NO LONGER JUST A "THIEF!"

He just turned **frustrated** or **psychotic** now wanting to:

- **HURT** your body!
- **TAKE YOUR LIFE!**

☑ **BREATHE!**

☑ **Physically FIGHT** (See Chapter 5)

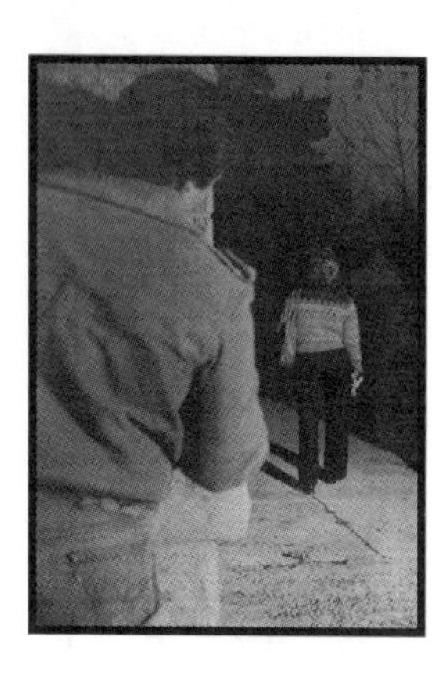

Preventing a ... FOLLOWING Attack

- React to your body's alarm system when it feels the **CREEPS**.
- React to **strange sounds** when you are walking alone.

*You already know to **walk** or **run** rapidly towards people for help when you are afraid. However, I know reality! Sometimes, through no fault of your own, safe places and safe people are not near you!*

Your safety is YOUR responsibility in a dangerous situtation. **TURN ORANGE!** Immediately show your courage and self-control:

☑ **BREATHE**! Grip and visualize LOVED ONES!
☑ **LOOK** around rapidly with **EYE-FIRE!**

Is someone FOLLOWING?

☑ **GLANCE** over your shoulders with eye-fire**, again** and **again.** You want your eyes to say: *"I know you are there!"*

☑ **MOVE your SPACE** by creating a ***bizarre*** **path**
... cross the street abruptly
... cut through moving traffic safely
... zig zag through parked cars in a lot
... walk around bushes, poles, trash cans, paper racks, etc.

☑ **KEEP WATCHING** the *threat* over your shoulder

The *threat* will likely give one of two responses:

- **He will GO AWAY!** Your behavior is too ridiculous and unpredictable. *You cannot prove what you STOPPED! Celebrate!!*

- **He will SPEED UP** and **FOLLOW** your bizarre path anyway!

☑ **KEEP BREATHING!**
☑ **RUN** if there is a safe place to go

OR ... if you are TRAPPED

☑ **TURN** at the stranger, before he's too close
☑ **LOOK** with eye-fire
☑ **POINT** your finger (declaring your SPACE)
☑ **CURSE** (speak RED to *stun* attacker)

... "What the FUCK do you want...?"
... "Get the HELL away from me...?"

When your life is in danger, you are **ALLOWED TO CURSE!** This outburst of RED acting requires **courage.** Remember, your loved ones are about to be attacked ... through your body!

> **If *vulgarity* stops violence ...**
> **then *vulgarity* = PEACE!**
> *Debbie Gardner*

If the attacker can comprehend the demonstration of your power, **HE WILL GO AWAY!**

If the attacker is incapable of comprehending your power because of hatred, drugs or alcohol intoxication, get ready!

HE WILL "CHARGE" AT YOU ANYWAY.

☑ **BREATHE** deeply as he approaches
☑ **PHYSICALLY *fight*** *(See Chapter 5)*

Preventing a ...
SURPRISE Attack

This is the worst style of attack, because there is no warning, and therefore little or no prevention possibilities. Whether you are walking, jogging, sleeping or just caught off-guard, please know your choices are limited:

- **Belly-ROAR** to activate your **BREATHING!**
- **Physically FIGHT** (See Chapter 5)

That's right! I recommend that you **Belly-ROAR** not SCREAM! Most people cannot scream in a crisis because screaming requires AIR in one's throat and neck. When you are terrified, there is no air in your throat or neck.

Many people have nightmares ... the traumatic experience of trying to "scream" in their dreams ... and no sound comes out. They wake up terrified with failure, and then make the faulty assumption that since they can't scream in their dreams, they probably can't scream in reality either! What negative conditioning!

> Turn on ESPN-TV and *listen* to million-dollar athletes! They never *scream* for power! They *roar* for power. *Roaring* tightens all your muscles and enhances your physical strength immediately! You have successfully moved something *heavy* ... because you *ROARED!*

Belly-ROARING can also:

- **Startle** your attacker
- **Draw** the attention of witnesses
- **Protect** your body from being "winded"
- **Protect** you from feeling pain ... until LATER!

STOP programming your body to respond to surprise fears by "holding your breath" and other "polite" responses.

START re-programming your body for self-control by belly-roaring whenever you are "surprise attacked" in non-violent, fearful tests!

"Paper cut" on your finger?	**ROAR** out your pain
Finger slammed in a door?	**ROAR** out your pain
Slip and fall to the ground?	**ROAR** out your pain
Winded by ball in the stomach?	**ROAR** out your pain
Face too deep in a hot oven?	**ROAR** out your pain
Startled by a scary movie	**ROAR** out your fear
Find a million dollar lottery ticket?	**ROAR** and call me!

This conscious practice is fun and can help your subconscious mind remember to **Belly-ROAR** instead of scream ... in your dreams and in reality!

Students have told me that **Belly-ROAR** practice actually put an end to their *freeze* nightmares!

TEARS from FEARS

In order to protect your personal **SPACE,** you now know you have the right to *lie, curse,* and *roar!*

As reasonable as those choices are, are you afraid you will fail ... because you have a history of CRYING uncontrollably when you are upset or afraid?

I understand. I was a "crier" too.

All those past fear-filled shortcomings occured because you and I stopped breathing or our breathing was shallow! You will be successful in the future because you now know to BREATHE, GRIP and visualize LOVED ONES which I promise will fight off those tears until ... **later!**

Yes, you can cry ... later! Crying is great ... after the crisis. *All successful soldiers cry ... later!* Tears cleanse the soul. Call me. I'll cry with you! I like criers. We have *heart.* The problem is ***inappropriately timed*** tears. Oh, celebration tears are wonderful, especially after successful completion of the battle!

I bet I know of a time when you stopped crying to *verbally control* yourself. Has something like this ever happened in your home:

> A family argument has just erupted. Everybody's feelings are hurt. Family members are crying and screaming. All of a sudden, the phone rings! Immediately, the bravest crier ... YOU ... quickly Belly-BREATHES, GRIPS the phone, and says "HELLO... o o o o!" as if there are no problems.

Your tears stopped immediately because you regained control of your oxygen, blood and positive thoughts by **breathing, gripping and pretending** *(to the caller from church, work, school)* that your family life is ... perfect!

If you relate to this story, GET EXCITED! You naturally have this skill, and you have successfully used it many times. Know that you **can** and **will** STOP TEARS to take control of your self **mentally** and **verbally** for crime prevention.

If crime prevention is not possible,
you **can** and **will** escalate to
save yourself **PHYSICALLY!**

SUMMARY of REMEMBER "S" for VERBAL CONTROL:

... Protect your **SPACE!**

Their Methods of Attack	*MY RESPONSE*
CONVERSATION (Distraction)	BREATHE...make Eye Contact Give NEGATIVE REPLY Step Back...holding Eye Contact
FOLLOWING	BREATHE...make Eye Contact Change path immediately Verbal Confrontation Vulgar Confrontation
SURPRISE	BREATHE ROAR!

Chapter Six

Remember "T"

Take Control Physically

You don't need many *physical* choices to save your life ... just **ONE** that works! What you really need are reasons to **justify** ... **ONE HIT!**

I know the thought of striking a human being is difficult, even to save your life. That's because fighting is RED ... and you are GOLDEN!

Just make me this promise: You will live your life assuming you ***can*** and ***will*...** instead of assuming you *can't* and *won't.* Remember: your motivation is LOVE, not hatred or anger.

Here are additional attitude adjustments to prepare your HEART for the choice to fight **physically.**

- **You have the *RIGHT* to physically fight for your BODY and your LIFE at all times!** *(When have you ever seen that phrase in print? NEVER? What a void! Believe it and teach it to your loved ones ... today!)*

I'd rather be tried by 12 than carried by 6

Remember. Fighting physically for property is **not** recommended. *A wallet may contain your life savings, but not your life!*

- A police officer is NOT going to jump out of the bushes and say "You are allowed to strike him now..." **PERMISSION to *strike* comes from a voice on the *inside* not the *outside* of your body.**

  Do you need an outsider's permission to save your loved one? Of course not! Your *inside voice* (HEART) gives you permission knowing when ***RIGHT ... is RIGHT!***

COURAGE

"Your heart's *natural wisdom* ...
telling you ***when*** and ***what*** to do ...
for the love of self and others."

Debbie Gardner

- **Hit with the intention to cause INJURY ... *not just pain.*** Assume your attacker feels no pain! Anyone who does not stop after your **m**ental and **v**erbal warnings is obviously "NUMB" from excessive drugs, alcohol or hatred.

- **HIT *FIRST ... when your SPACE LINE is invaded.*** This choice guarantees you ONE strike to STOP your assailant immediately!

  The law allows you to use self-defense to defend against:

  - physical harm
  - the THREAT of physical harm
  - serious physical harm
  - the THREAT of serious physical harm
  - death

Visualize THREAT of physical or serious physical harm as *unstoppable SPACE invasion,* especially after you have done all in your power to "step back" while delivering verbal commands.

BEWARE

of the accidental influence of the phrase:
FIGHT BACK!

Do not allow your logical mind to assume that you must be struck first ... before you are allowed to "fight BACK." No! Self-defense laws do NOT require you to receive a hit ... **before** you are allowed to **hit**. Besides, if you were *struck first* ... do you really believe you could immediately recover and effectively "fight BACK?"

Hitting *first* does NOT make you the aggressor. The attacker is the aggressor coming after YOU. You are simply defending your trapped space by fighting right ... and **hitting *first!***

When an attacker approaches, control yourself ***mentally*** ... then turn ORANGE ***verbally*** to protect your SPACE non-violently:

- ☑ **BREATHE! GRIP** and visualize **LOVED ONES!**
- ☑ **LIE! ... CURSE! ... ROAR!**

If the attacker does not stop ... turn **RED** as you:

- ☑ **Strike the THROAT ... then RUN!**

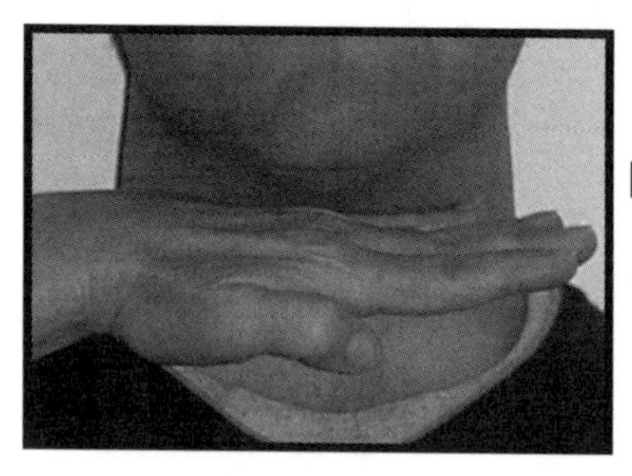

"T" of "BST" reminds you to STRIKE the THROAT!

Go for the **THROAT** with BOTH Hands

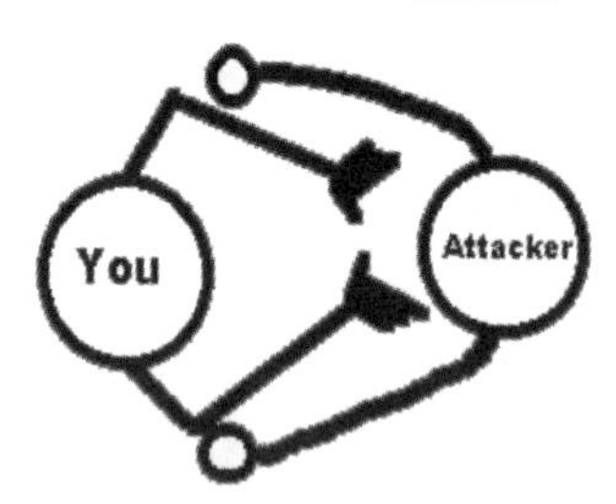

Either one of your arms may "accidently" block a sudden attack within your Space!

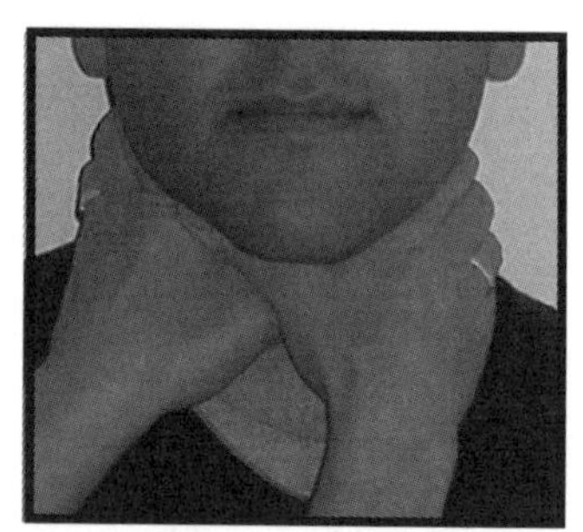

Concentrate pressure on the **throat** not the whole neck!

Your goal is to ***"Take his BREATH away!"*** If he is not ***breathing,*** he cannot continue to attack you, regardless of his size advantage or level of intoxication.

HOW TO PRACTICE

I believe effective crime survival requires the repetition of ***internal*** practice (permission statements, positive visualization, righteous beliefs, etc.) more so than ***external*** (physical) practice.

Perfect *technique* is not your goal. Stopping *air* is your goal. Your arm and hand movements are minimal! ***Striking the THROAT*** is similar to *reaching for a can of soda* in your refrigerator:

Reach in ... strike (grab) ... pull out

The issue is not ***CAN*** *you strike the THROAT "properly"*
The issue is ***WILL*** *you strike the THROAT ... "first!"*

> **"Self Defense is about COURAGE, not KARATE!"**
> *Debbie Gardner*

You are probably concerned with a few valid issues:

1. ***How do I make sure I'll remember ... THROAT?***
   ANSWER: You will remember because it is too simple to forget! And, I am going to assign you life-long *practice* homework that is *fun*!

2. **How *hard* do I need to *strike* to cause injury?**
   ANSWER: Not much force is needed ... which brings up an important problem. You may NOT practice *STRIKE the THROAT* on co-workers, family members, friends, etc. ... because it works!

   A slight *strike to the THROAT* can cause immediate choking. A strong strike or "grab" of the THROAT "tube" can cause serious injury and even death! This is a RED, desperate choice to be used in a *life or death scenario* only.

3. How do I use my hand(s) to *strike* properly?

ANSWER: A punch with your fist is **not recommended**! It creates too *fat* of a weapon. Some attackers don't have *necks* large enough for fists to fit into!

The **BST** hand position is a **tight, flat, open hand(s)** ... *slicing* at the THROAT. The motion, whether used forward or backward will look like a *karate chop* if just one hand is used!

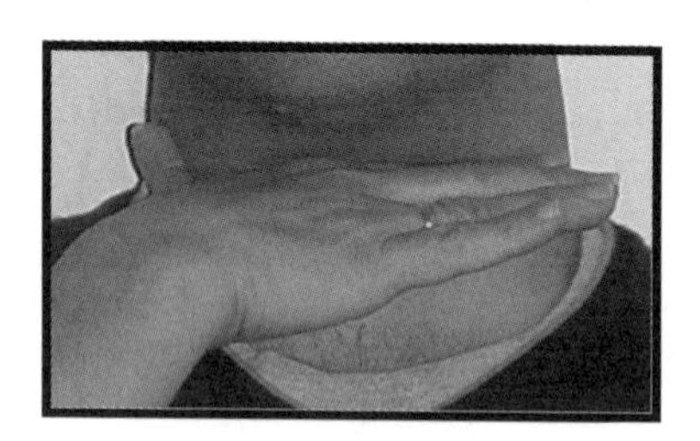

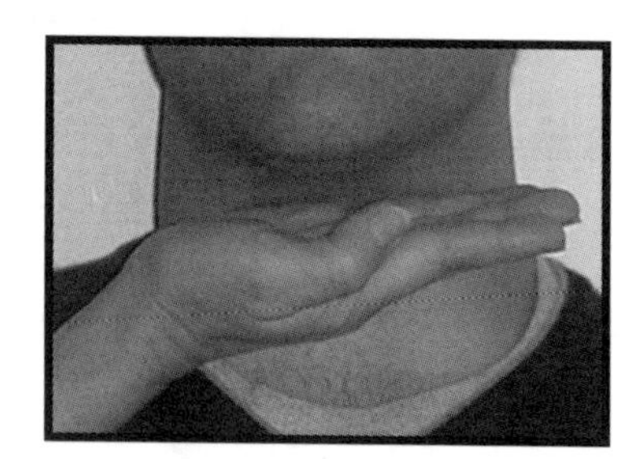

4. What about hitting the GROIN, EYES or NOSE?

ANSWER: Those choices are not wrong, just NOT the **BST**!

- Striking the GROIN usually just **hurts** men who **feel pain.** *If your assailant does not "feel" because of an excessive amount of hatred, drugs, and/or alcohol in his system ... your guaranteed ONE STRIKE ... is a miss!* It is very hard for untrained people to cause serious incapacitating injury to the groin. If your guaranteed ONE STRIKE fails to STOP your assailant, and in fact makes him *madder* ... the physical violence against you will greatly intensify.

Exception: For those looking for an ORANGE physical defense in a circumstance that has not yet escalated to RED (like *pending* **date rape**) a strike to the *groin* may be used as a reasonable *lesser* physical option to *STOP* an aroused, *sober* date. To stop an aroused, *intoxicated* date who is using force to attempt sexual assault ... a RED choice (hit the THROAT) is needed because an ORANGE choice is not likely to be felt.

- A strike to the *eyes* and *nose* can cause incapacitating injury if it delivered with **extreme** force. PROBLEM: Most GOLDEN people question their emotional ability to gouge the eyes or smash the nose ... because of their discomfort touching the assailant's body fluid with their hands!

I conduct an interesting test regularly, when speaking to hundreds of men and women in large corporate audiences. I ask:

"...How many of you already KNOW to *gouge the eyes* or *smash the nose?"*
Almost 100% of the audience raises their hand!

"...How many of you, however, have a little voice in your heart that says: 'Yuk!!! But I probably COULDN'T or WOULDN'T...?'"
Almost 100% of the audience raises their hand again!

"...Is it because of your fear of getting the attackers eye or nose **body fluid** on your hands?"
Yes! is the unanimous response.

"... In comparison, does hitting the THROAT bother you at all?"
No! is the near unanimous response.

Bottom Line:
Maybe you have had extensive military, police or self-defense training and therefore have no emotional hesitation connected to striking the eyes or nose. That's great!

Maybe your strike to the groin will work ... and maybe it won't! Those 50/50 odds do not represent the **BST** choice for my family or me in a life-saving struggle. You have the right, however to disagree and make your own crime survival plan: <u>BSG</u>roin? <u>BSE</u>yes? <u>BSN</u>ose?

I choose to consider THROAT as **BST** for two additional reasons:

1) How many animals fight for their life by attacking their opponent's groin? Eyes? Nose? **None!** How many animals kill ... going for their opponent's THROAT? **Many!**

2) In a first-aid rescue, life-saving choices are offered in this A-B-C order of **importance**:

Check the **<u>A</u>IR**
Check the <u>**B**</u>LEEDING
Check <u>**C**</u>IRCULATION

★ When our son was 10 years old, he made a great recommendation after watching a seminar. Instead of using the word *slice* to describe striking the THROAT, Jimmy suggested that I say, ***"Hit with <u>LOVE</u>"*** ... demonstrating that a hand actually looks like the letter "L" when striking the THROAT!

- The thumb-side of a hand looks like a capital "L" when the thumb sticks out
- The backside of a hand looks like a lowercase "l" when a hand is tight.

Jim also observed that two hands create "4-LOVES" (2 uppercase "L's" and 2 lowercase "l's"... *Only 4th graders think about these things!)* He suggested that since a criminal only has ONE throat, your odds of striking effectively are 4 to 1. Roaring out the word ***"LOVE!"*** as you hit, was also his *(comical)* idea.

I was stunned by his heart warming metaphor! I immediately adopted his suggestion to show my hand position as the letter "L" in order to **"Hit with LOVE"** and ... I encourage you to think of it this way, too. It helps *soften* ownership of a very frightening, yet valuable life-saving choice.

I hope you will take the hand position of *"L" = LOVE* a step further. When you leave your loved ones, wave good-bye with your **LOVE hand-position** (which looks a lot like a "high-five.") It will remind them of their rights and natural power every time they leave home.

I am honored when people recognize me in public places and shout out *"Hey Debbie ... how are you?"* then raise up their ***LOVE hand*** which tells me they were in my class somewhere ... and *remember* the **BST** message!

These Ninth Grade girls saw our seminar when they were in the Sixth Grade. Three years later they recognized me at a football game and said, "You're that BREATHE Lady," as they held up their dangerous "L = LOVE" hands!

They made my day because they remembered a life-saving concept with a smile on their face!

HOMEWORK ASSIGNMENT

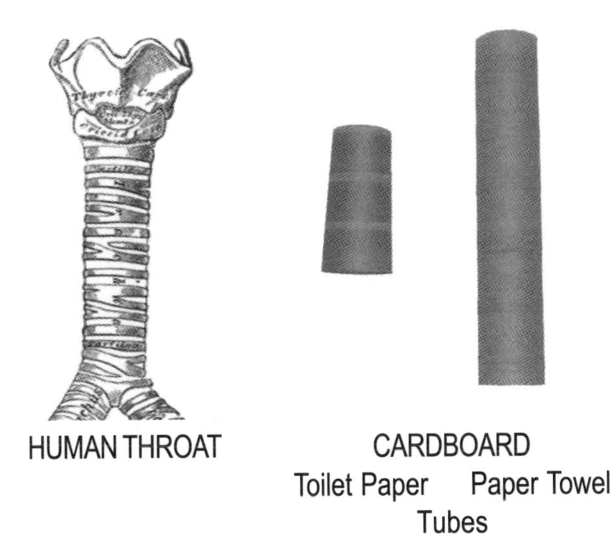

HUMAN THROAT

CARDBOARD
Toilet Paper Paper Towel
Tubes

The human throat is a very *frail* organ. Like the cardboard tube that supports a roll of paper towels or toilet paper rolls, the *walls* of the human throat collapse easily when struck.

For the *rest of your life*, whenever you come across a cardboard paper towel or toilet paper tube, hold it in the center of one hand and **strike** it with your other "L = LOVE" hand, **roaring** with force. Then smile as you remind yourself *"for my loved ones I can do anything."*

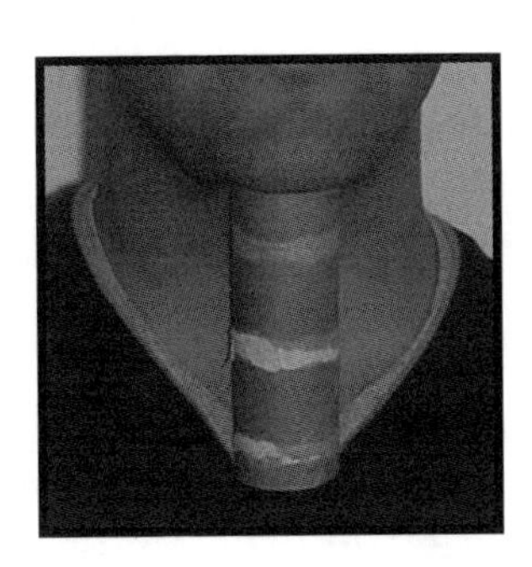

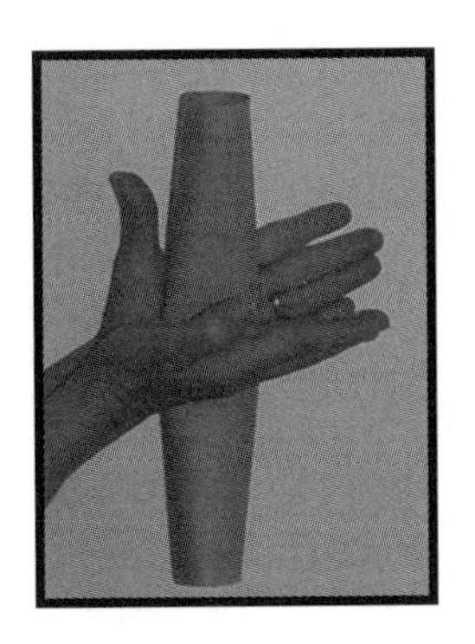

- Be sure that your family members take turns striking *cardboard THROATS*. Our daughter has been roaring and striking *cardboard THROATS* regularly since she was 8 years old. She is now a college graduate. What are the odds of her forgetting ONE realistic life-saving skill?

- When a cardboardpaper towel tube appears at a party ... strike it with your "L = LOVE" hand, and explain what you just did to all in the kitchen with you. Parties are wonderful places to rapidly teach your **BST** beliefs. Make sure everyone takes a turn striking the cardboard *THROAT*. Keep the dialogue light and fun as you inspire people with ONE idea that is so memorable, it might just save their life someday!

- SUCCESS STORY! Years ago, a young high school teacher called me with a touching "Christmas Empowerment Story" that occurred in her family.

  Months before Christmas that year, the young teacher survived a brutal rape by a man who *jumped* her as she was locking the door of her high school after an evening music event. The school administrators later sponsored our evening seminar in celebration of her courage and survival.

  After the holidays, this brave survivor called me to describe an event that occurred while opening Christmas presents after midnight church services that Christmas Eve. Her young 12 year-old sister (*who had attended our seminar with the survivor's entire family*) insisted that their mother open her very special, large present ***FIRST***. The adult family members were curious about this large present because their young sister had no money ... and no one took her shopping. The entire family was anxious to see what was in the surprise package that made the little sister so proud.

As the mother opened the gift, she gently started to cry as she read a note that accompanied a department store box filled with dozens of ...

CRUSHED CARDBOARD PAPER TOWEL TUBES!

The note read...
"Mom, I just want you to know ... I AM READY"
I love you...

As the teacher said those words to me over the phone, we both struggled with awkward silence to *breathe-back tears.* Continuing the story, she reported her whole family broke down and cried through their smiles as the meaning behind her sister's gift of *crushed paper towel tubes* became evident. The 12 year-olds Christmas gift was a symbol of courage and preparedness so that "Mom wouldn't worry about me *(my safety)* ... as I grow up."

To think that this precious child thought to use my *corny* "paper-towel tube = THROAT" idea to express complex feelings of pain, pride and power to her family ... made me feel so honored. I remain indebted to this wonderful teacher for taking the time to share her family's evening of empowerment and peace with me.

Most Valuable Player

Like any other serious problem in life, it isn't just *what* you do, but ***how you explain*** what you did. Use the meaning of

MVP

as your guide to explain your **BST** choices to the police, detectives, juries and judges:

Example:

"Judge, I have the **right** to work late ... and walk to my car alone. I felt something was wrong. So instantly I **breathed deeply, gripped** my keys and **thought of my children** for inspiration.
*(**M**ental Control)*

I **looked** behind me, and saw the defendant walking quickly towards me. There was no place to run. No people around. I kept my **eyes** on him as I began to make a bizarre path around others people's cars. I hoped he would think I was nuts and go away. He didn't. He rushed towards my **space.** I pointed my finger at him and said: ***"Get the F_ away from me!"***
*(**V**erbal Control)*

He didn't stop. In fact he didn't even act like he heard me. His eyes were weird. Trapped up against my car, **I HIT HIM** when he crossed into my personal space. I had no choice but to defend myself and take control of the situation. If he had hit me first, I probably would not be here today. As you can see, he is twice my size. I did the minimum to save my life."
*(**P**hysical Control)*

SUMMARY of REMEMBER "T" for PHYSICAL CONTROL

- **"T"** of the **BST** message = Strike the **THROAT!**
- **Hit first** to defend your trapped space
- Cause **injury**
- Practice striking ***cardboard*** from paper towel and toilet paper ***"tubes"***
- **ROAR** as your STRIKE
- Teach your **BST** crime survival message to loved ones and friends at parties, especially when "tubes" appear!

Breathe
Space
Throat

- Use **MVP** to *explain* your **M**ental, **V**erbal then **P**hysical choices.

Think like a peak-performance athlete for a minute. Decide:

CRIME SURVIVAL is simple.
It is about "OXYGEN!"

You need ***your*** **AIR** to play...
You need to take ***your opponent's*** **AIR** to win!

THREAT

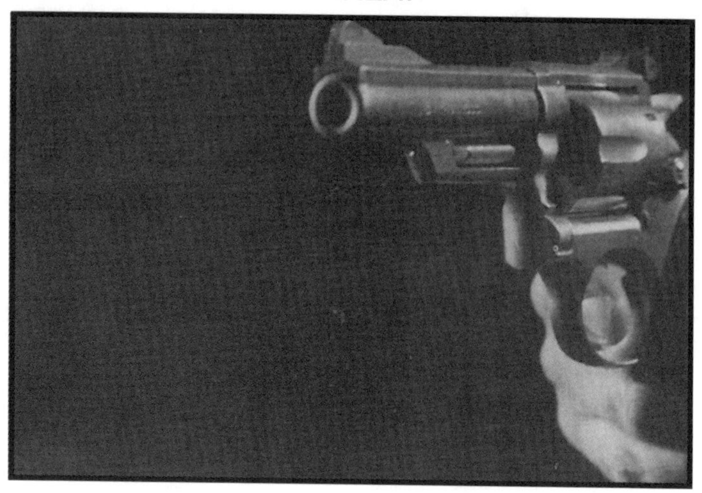

WEAPON

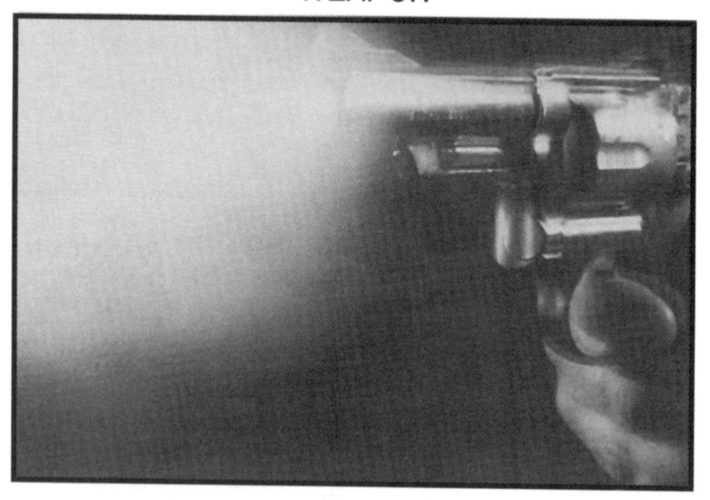

Chapter Seven

Weapon Survival

This chapter is extremely important. Please read it carefully. Then reread it to insure that you fully understand the principles of confronting an armed attacker. By no means is this chapter intended to provide elaborate instructions, such as what the Secret Service uses to protect the President or Heads of State.

My goal is to arm you, a law-abiding GOLDEN person, with a few solid principles that you can recall easily and use effectively to *improve your odds* of surviving an armed assailant, because these odds are NOT acceptable:

Attacker – 100 Law-abiding citizen – 0

THREAT or WEAPON?

The sight of a weapon is going to *take your BREATH away!* **Control yourself:**

☑ **BREATHE!** Grip! Visualize LOVED ONES!

Immediately determine whether the weapon is being used as a THREAT or a WEAPON. Is there a difference? You bet there is!

When a robber aims a gun at a store clerk and says. "Give me all the money or I'll shoot you," the gun at that point is being used just as a **THREAT**. He is using the gun as ***underlying force*** to get what he wants ... MONEY! The robber knows if he walked up to the counter unarmed, shaking his fist at the clerk while demanding money, the clerk would not take him seriously. Therefore, the robber arms himself with a gun or a knife to prove that he is serious and also to frighten the clerk into complying with his demands. In this example, the robber has no intention of using that gun to hurt the clerk; he only wants the money. The gun is being used as a THREAT, not as a WEAPON! It is important that the store clerk gain control of himself (BREATHE, Grip, Visualize LOVED ONES) and **comply** with the robber's demands because when an armed thief is ..."happy" ... he usually goes away.

If the armed thief escalates his anger and is "UN-happy" ... because there is not enough money or property, and/ or if the attacker walks in the store **FRUSTRATED** wanting to injure the body of the clerk (physically or sexually) the weapon continues to be a THREAT for the clerk to ***comply.***

If the armed attacker comes into the store, disoriented and enraged, walks right past the open cash drawer, shoots a customer, then pushes the store clerk into the back room, it is reasonable to assume that the gun is about to be used as a WEAPON to *kill* the clerk. This is especially evident if the attacker ***ignores*** pleas from the clerk to take the store's money and all the possessions he wants. At this point, the clerk has nothing to lose by **trying** to save his own life.

With *basic weapon survival* principles, the clerk can substantially increase his odds of surviving ... but NEVER will his survival odds increase to 50/50; that is impossible when an attacker is armed and a clerk (or any GOLDEN person) is not!

NEVER, NEVER, NEVER, NEVER, NEVER, NEVER, NEVER, NEVER,
NEVER, NEVER, NEVER, NEVER, NEVER, NEVER, NEVER, NEVER,
NEVER, NEVER, NEVER, NEVER, NEVER, NEVER, NEVER, NEVER,
NEVER, NEVER, NEVER, NEVER, NEVER, NEVER, NEVER, NEVER,

NEVER

let an attacker, especially an "armed" attacker, move you ...

... from where the attack started: **CRIME SCENE "A"**
... to another location: **CRIME SCENE "B"**
(like a woods, car trunk, house, etc.)

The reason a criminal wants to MOVE you is because **he is AFRAID of being CAUGHT at SCENE "A."** Whether you decide to ...

1) *give up* property
2) *comply* to body abuse
3) *fight* for your life

... do it where the attacker ***declares fear***...
CRIME SCENE "A!"

Fight rather than be moved, even if he threatens to *kill* you if you don't move. The **BST** odds of survival exist at **CRIME SCENE "A."**

PLEASE, NEVER ALLOW AN ATTACKER TO MOVE YOU!

All crime survival choices *stink*. Like reaching to find something inside a smelly trash can, crime survival choices smell at different levels of danger. *Weapon survival stinks* the most because all options are very dangerous.

ARMED ATTACKERS WANT THREE THINGS:

1) PROPERTY ... Give it up with no resistance!

2) YOUR BODY (physical or sexual assault)

PRETEND to COMPLY in order to

- Catch your breath in order to TALK,NEGOTIATE
- Catch the attention of others with NOISE
- Catch your moment to FIGHT *RIGHT*

COMPLY to save your life!

I am convinced from countless conversations with rape survivors, that many do not make a *choice* to comply, but rather have no choice because they have NO AIR ... due to physical force or extreme terror. By the time survivors start to BREATHE, sexual assault is already in progress. That is when survivors decide: *"I just want this over with. Fighting (or resisting) will just make it worse."*

- If the sacrifice of your body ... saves your life ... then **complying is honorable!** Do not second-guess your desperate life-saving choice.

- A rapist might promise if you comply, he will not kill you. Remember that rapists, like all criminals, are LIARS! Pretend to trust as you keep searching for options to escape or fight effectively. Tragically, some rapists kill anyway.

FIGHT!

- If attacker's rage heightens after rape
- If you have AIR and
  detest the thought of being raped

3) YOUR LIFE ...*FIGHT physically*

SURVIVOR'S EVIDENCE TRIANGLE

Overwhelmed by unstoppable violence, an attacker may have control of your body, but not your *mind*! **Be sure to TAKE and LEAVE evidence!** For emotional control ... think, *"You've got me now, I'll get you later ... in court."* Look forward to telling detectives about the evidence you deliberately gathered to build your case. Remember to:

LEAVE from YOU: hair, clothing fibers, fingernail tips, jewelry, buttons, shoes, etc. Tuck these items into his pockets and clothing and all over the environment. TOUCH and leave your fingerprints everywhere. SCRATCH your initials or license number into furniture, dirt, and car seat, etc.

TAKE from the ATTACKER: hair, clothing fibers, buttons, etc. *Hide them in your mouth.* Get his sweat and blood on your clothing. Claw his skin with your fingernails.

TAKE from ENVIRONMENT: grass, pebbles, carpet fiber, car seat fabric, shrubbery, dirt, etc. Put this evidence on your attacker including down his pockets and waistband! Put this evidence on you, especially in your pockets and your *mouth.* Your mouth is a secure holding place for small items that will be collected in the emergency room.

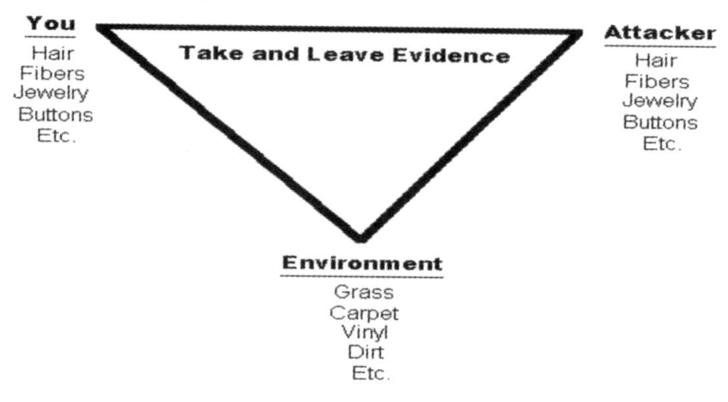

SURVIVING A GUN ATTACK

If violence continues after your ***property*** and ***body*** have been offered or sacrificed, then all that is left for the attacker to take is your **LIFE!**

- ☑ **BREATHE!** Grip! Visualize LOVED ONES!
- ☑ **PUT UP YOUR ARMS** in a surrender position and if you can, **ASK "What do you want..."** Make a final attempt to negotiate options. Assume the gun is going to ***fire!***

The question is, *where does the bullet go*? Remember, bullets kill people, not guns (unless the gun is used as a *beating* instrument.) Bullets come out of the **barrel** of the gun. **The direction of the barrel determines your life or death,** because the barrel creates the **bullet's path**.

You will likely survive a bullet shot in your shoulder, arms, hands, buttocks, legs and feet.

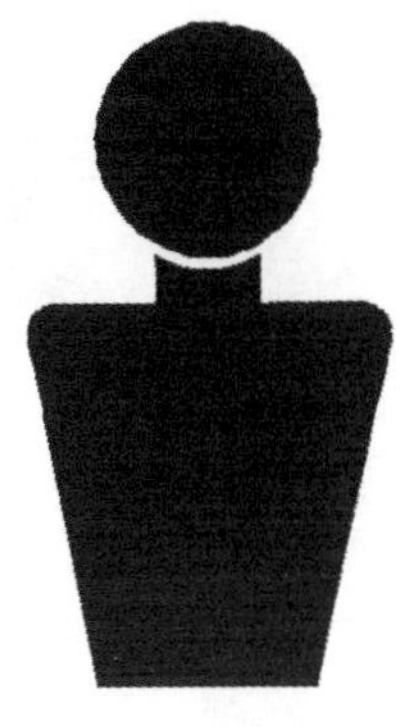

KILL ZONE

You are NOT likely to survive a bullet shot in your **KILL ZONE** which includes your head, neck, chest and stomach.

It is critical that you do all in your power to keep bullets from striking your **KILL ZONE!**

How far away is the attacker? It is *good if he is close* and the gun is within your *forward* reach. If the gun is in an awkward place like your back, your response will be more difficult, so:

☑ **PRETEND to be afraid** ... it's easy!

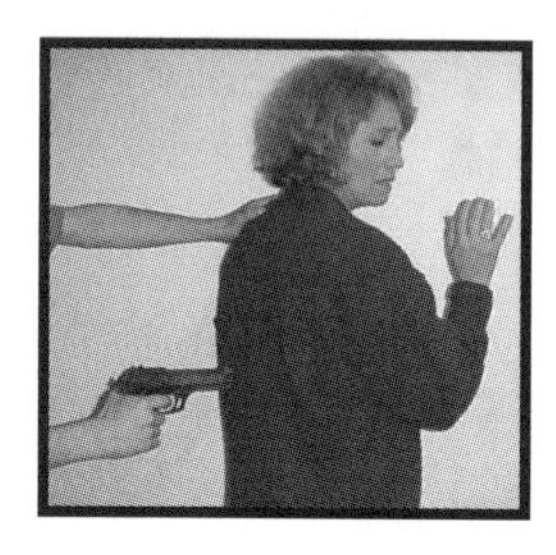
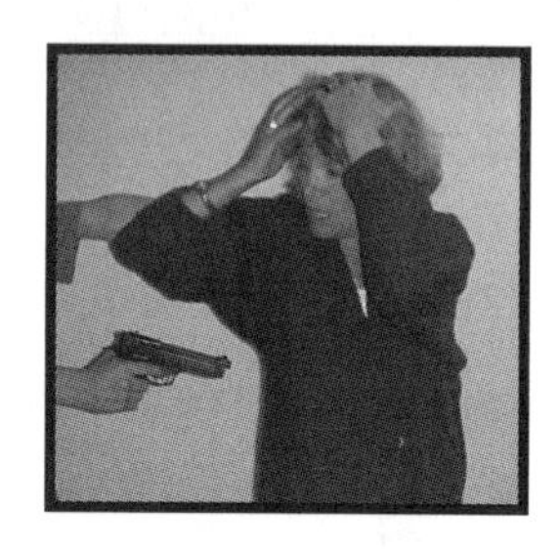
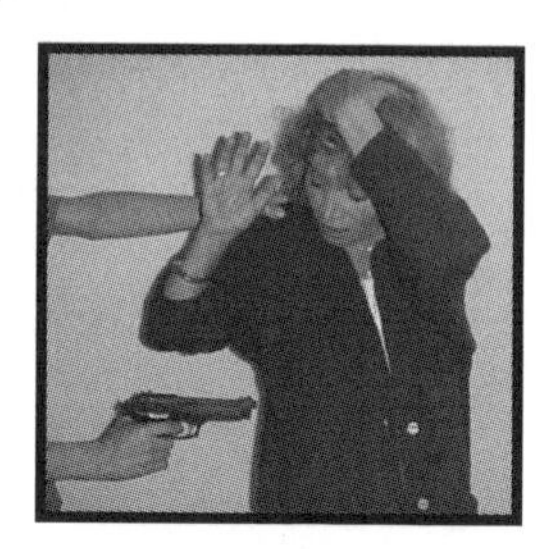

Shaking your head and twisting your body in a *nervous* way will allow you to better SEE the gun and possibly shift its location from the *center of your back* to the *side of your back* ... which is an improved position for your physical struggle. Even if there is violent, threatening language like: *"Don't move! Look straight ahead!"* ... **act afraid and squirm around**. This defiance is risky, yet if successful, can greatly improve your position to fight effectively. Then:

☑ **GRAB and REDIRECT the gun BARREL**
☑ **Strike the THROAT ... and RUN!**

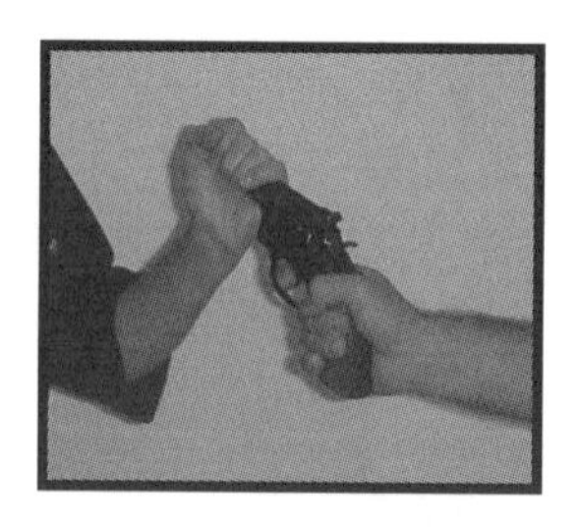
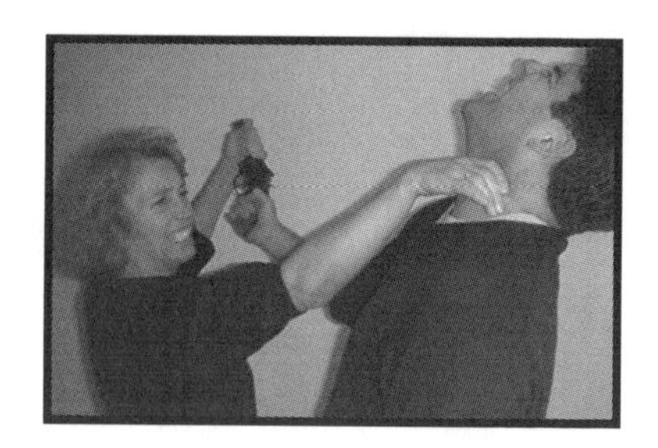

EXPLANATION:

GRAB with whichever hand is closest to the barrel of the gun, **moving the barrel up, down or to either side ...** whatever is the quickest direction away from your KILL ZONE.

- **Do not try to *wrestle* the gun *away*.** Taking the gun away is not your goal. You just want the barrel (*and bullets*) moved immediately from your KILL ZONE because the gun is going to *fire!*

  Example: If fired, a gun barrel *(and bullets)* aimed at your heart is DEATH. If fired, a gun barrel *(and bullets)* grabbed and redirected down towards your hip is probably LIFE.

- **Injury will occur.** Your hand that *grabs* the gun barrel will likely be:

  BURNED by the heat of the gun firing
  RIPPED-UP by gun chamber movement
  SHOT if your hand grabs the end of the barrel

  In other words, you need to **choose injury** to **save your KILL ZONE**. Would you easily *choose injury* to your hand to *save a loved one*? Of course!

STRIKE THE THROAT as soon as possible with your *other* hand. If the attacker stops *breathing*, he cannot keep firing the gun! RUN! Take the gun if you can!

- If trapped in an odd position with only one hand free to react, what do you think is the **BST** choice?

GRAB the gun barrel?
or
Strike the **THROAT**?

Absolutely, GRAB the gun BARREL FIRST to save your KILL ZONE! Then, strike the THROAT as soon as possible! Always assume the gun will fire immediately and keep firing. Move the bullets out of your KILL ZONE at any cost to your hands and arms.

Fascinating GUN SURVIVAL ideas that require *courage!*

- ❖ Your attacker's force is likely to **drag you to the ground.** That is OK! The fighting principles (**GRAB** the barrel – Strike the **THROAT**) remain the same when rolling around on the ground. Keep roaring for AIR!

- ❖ As long as you keep the gun barrel aimed away from your KILL ZONE ... your life is saved even though the gun is firing and your gun-grabbing hand is severely injured. Your body will go into *shock* which means you are ***not likely* to *feel* the pain** of your hand injury or any injury ... until many seconds or minutes after the attack ends.

> *"No champion is embarassed by his scars"*
> H. Jackson Brown

❖ **LARGE barreled guns,** *although frightening to see,* are the easiest barrels to **GRAB and REDIRECT!** Small guns with short barrels are hard to see and difficult to GRAB.

❖ **It is good if a gun is shoved into your body** ... because it is likely the *barrel* is within your *reach* to GRAB and redirect! When a gun barrel is **INSIDE your SPACE,** your odds of surviving are greatly improved!

❖ If the attacker holds the gun **OUTSIDE of your SPACE, your odds of surviving have dropped dramatically** because you cannot GRAB the gun barrel and *move* the bullets. This style of attack is technically an "assassination" with extremely low odds of survival. If a gunman hides completely and shoots from a long distance, you have **no chance** to save yourself! Example: Drive-by shooting.

❖ If a gunman confronts you from just a few feet **OUTSIDE of your SPACE**, you have a small window of opportunity to save yourself. Example: Workplace violence

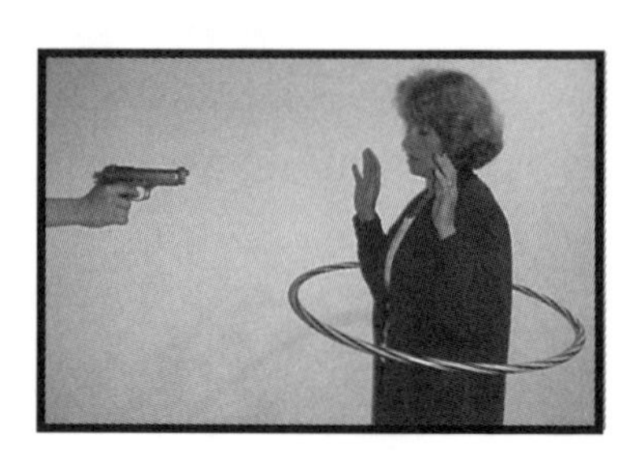

☑ **BREATHE!** Grip! Visualize LOVED ONES!

☑ Put your **HANDS UP in front of your head**. Appear as if you are *wringing your head* in nervousness. The bones in your arms might protect your head and neck from bullets. Keep one elbow over your *heart* area for protection.

☑ **"LIE WITH LOVE!"** Use *loving* and *agreeing* words to NURTURE and distract his mind. It would be great if you could negotiate with him to *put the gun down*!

AVOID using the phrase *"I understand..."* In crisis dialogue, that phrase tends to infuriate *violent* people. They feel their pain is unique, only experienced by them! A better repetitive phrase to nurture a violent person is: *"Yes, **I HEAR you**. OK! You're RIGHT. **I HEAR you!"***

☑ **STEP TOWARDS HIM carefully!** Yes, he can shoot you at any time because *you are moving in close.* He can also shoot you if you just *stay where you are and do nothing!* In this desperate *assassination* setting, you have nothing to lose by **moving slowly** into his space in an attempt to **GRAB** and redirect the gun barrel.

If he becomes **startled** by someone or something ... you need to react immediately:

☑ **LUNGE towards the gun BARREL, attempting to GRAB and REDIRECT** it with *one* or *both* hands. The gun is firing! You need to keep the bullets away from your KILL *ZONE (and maybe the KILL ZONE of others.)* As soon as possible, release one of your two hands from the gun barrel and ...

☑ Strike the **THROAT** to **STOP** the gunman. **RUN!**

BULLET PROOF "PAPER" VESTS! A large stack of compressed paper is likely to stop or significantly slow down the impact of bullets fired at your KILL ZONE from a distance!

In an office, on a plane, in school ... GRAB books, magazines, file folders or stack of paper items that gives you a large GRIP of at least 5" to 6" of compressed paper! City phone books and school bags filled with texts books have the potential to save your life.

☑ **Hold up books** up to protect your *front* KILL ZONE; use a **book bag** to protect your *back* KILL ZONE.

- RUN away *(in a zigzag path)* from gunfire. Take cover *outside* behind the engine of a parked car with your feet protected by a front tire.

☑ **Charge towards** a gunman's **barrel** if you are *trapped* and facing unpreventable *assassination.*

- Use books or book bag as a **SHIELD** to protect your KILL ZONE
- Knock the **BARREL (and bullets) DOWN** with books and/or GRAB the gun barrel with your hand
- Strike the **THROAT**!

5" - 6" of paper in school bag

3 books stopped 9mm, 357 mag, and 44 mag bullets from 10 feet

SURVIVING A KNIFE ATTACK ...

or any weapon that cuts or stabs, such as box-cutters, ice picks, razors, broken bottles, etc.

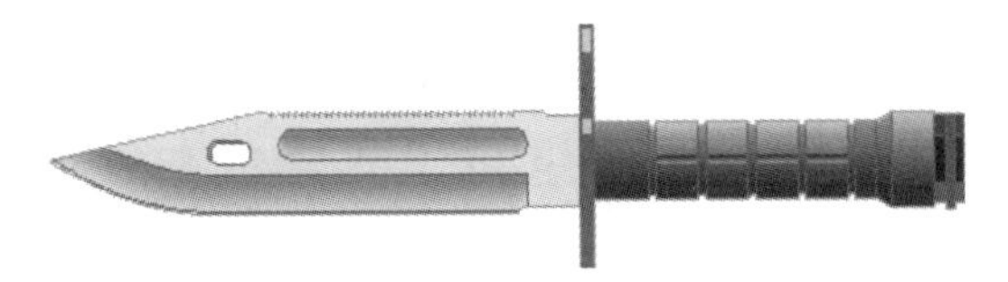

STOP! Put this book down. If you are over 18 *(or under 18 with the permission of a parent)* go to the kitchen and pick out a variety of knives ... of various size and sharpness!

No, I am not kidding. This is important!

RESPECTFULLY, pick up the dullest knife and lay it in the palm of your hand. Grab the knife by the blade and squeeze gently. Repeat with each knife you have selected, from dullest to sharpest.

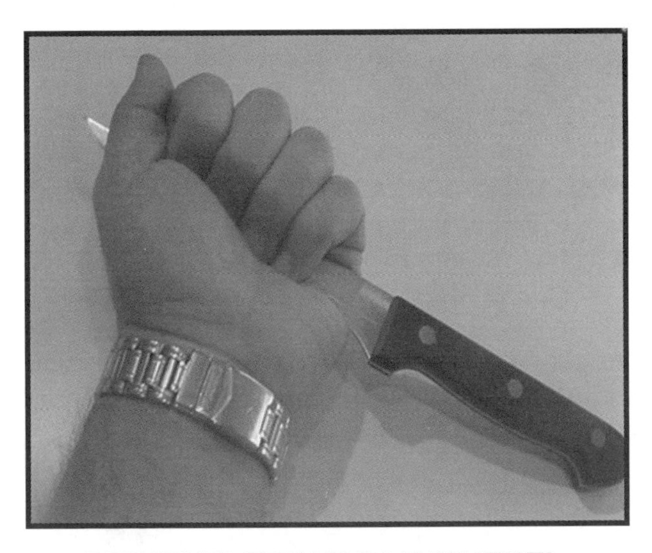

BREATHE! BREATHE! BREATHE!

Do you have knife phobia?

Pay attention to the beat of your heart. Is it racing? Are you saying negative things to yourself like ... "No way! I CAN'T DO THIS!" If just the *thought* or the *sight* of a sharp blade touching your skin causes shortness of breath and a pounding heart ... you have **knife phobia,** a programmed *inside* monster you need to conquer.

If you are terrified to touch the blade of a knife in a ***safe*** setting, what are your odds of self-control and knife survival if you are attacked?

Don't take me out of context! It is reasonable for people to respect the cutting power of knives for everyday safety. It is NOT reasonable, however, for people to "FREEZE in a crime" because they allow the influence of vivid mental monsters to magnify the negative consequences of GRABBING a knife by the blade.

STOP visualizing extreme, bizarre injuries! Yes, your hand will receive nasty, repairable cuts. NO! Your hands and fingers are not likely to be *"cut off"* landing in a pool of blood that drowns the neighborhood!

Imagine how poorly you would drive if you allowed mental monsters to vividly picture a "head-on" collision every time you turned "left!"

What would happen if you vividly pictured a vicious cut on your throat or leg every time you SHAVED with a sharp razor blade!

What you focus on ... expands! Example: *If you focus your thoughts on the taste of a crisp, cold pickle ... you'll be eating one within an hour!*

In a similar way, you can choose to be positive and change your ***knife phobia*** to ***knife respect.*** Focus on the possibility that you *can* and *will* **TRY** to save your life by GRABBING a knife by the blade ... if challenged in a desperate situation.

Practice your "***WILL-power***" regularly! Respectfully place and gently squeeze the blades of knives in your hands when you do the dishes. BREATHE deeply, and say to yourself. *"For my loved ones, I will TRY ..."* Do this until you no longer experience rapid heart beats and shortness of breath when touching a sharp blade against your skin. Commit to breaking your phobia (negative thinking) NOW! *Teach loved ones to break this phobia, too. It is very common!*

If "trapped" with unpreventable violence from a KNIFE-wielding attacker who is determined to destroy your LIFE, follow a plan similar to your worst-case scenario gun defense:

- ☑ **BREATHE!** Grip! Visualize LOVED ONES!
- ☑ **PUT UP YOUR ARMS** in a *surrender position* and if you can, ASK "What do you want..." Make a final attempt to negotiate options. Accept reality ... you are going to be cut! ***You decide WHERE!***
- ☑ **GRAB the knife by the BLADE!**
- ☑ **Strike the THROAT ... and RUN!**

Fascinating KNIFE SURVIVAL ideas that require *courage!*

- When you GRAB a knife by the blade, **squeeze the blade as tightly as possible!** Yes, even with a tight GRIP, it is likely you are going to get cut and bleed. Faced with a determined, armed attacker, you are going to get cut and bleed anyway! You need to choose which part of your of your body bleeds ... your hand(s) ... or your heart? Neck? Chest?

- The **TIGHTER YOU GRAB** the knife, the *less it will move* in your hand, and the ***less it will cut*** your hand. Avoiding a cut completely is not likely. By contrast, a loose grip will allow the blade to move more and cut more.

- If the thought of **protecting your GRAB HAND** with fabric from the sleeve of your clothing or any other reachable item (like a magazine) helps you have the *courage to TRY* ...GO FOR IT! In reality, you may not have the time to arrange protection for your hand.

- **Trainers!** If you feel you can **BLOCK the knife** with a memorized blocking motion ... go ahead. I am willing to admit I never believed blocks would work for me! Police work taught me reality. There is a huge difference between the **predictable** pattern of knife-blocking practice in a gym and the **unpredictable** behavior of violent street criminals.

- Remember, in a worse case scenario, a severely injured hand can usually be **repaired or replaced.** A severely injured neck or heart ... usually cannot!

- ❖ Would you be willing to sacrifice your hand(s) to defend the heart, neck or chest of your loved ones? Of course! WOW! Doing it for "LOVED ONES" always increases your optimism!

Please ... make sure *your name* is at
the top of your **"Loved Ones" LIST**!

If attacked from BEHIND with a KNIFE in your NECK

- ☑ **BREATHE/ROAR** Visualize LOVED ONES!
- ☑ **GRAB the BLADE TIGHTLY!**
- ☑ **PULL the blade off your neck.** If the blade is going to cut something, decide it will be your hand(s)!
- ☑ **TURN** even if falling.
- ☑ **Strike the THROAT** as soon as possible. **RUN!**

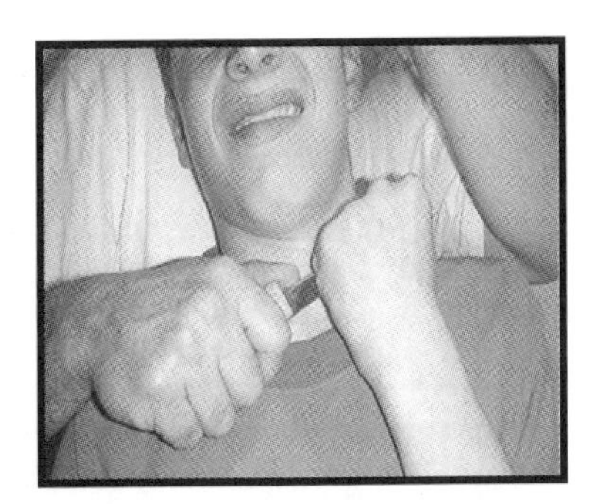

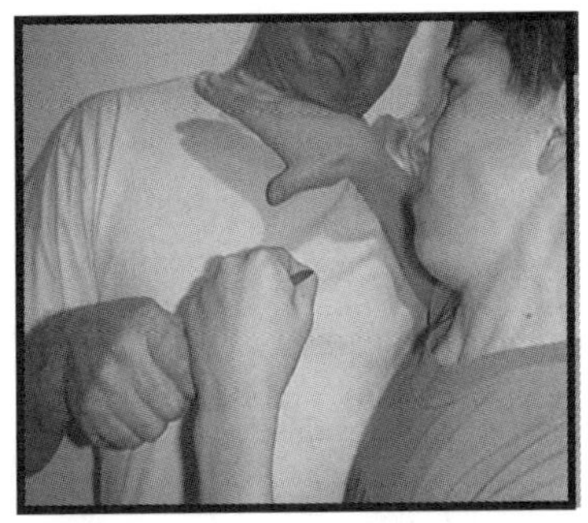

***BAR LEVERAGE* is on your side!** You need very little strength or *muscle power* to pull the end of the blade off your neck *if* you have the courage to grab the BLADE with your HAND!

RESIST the temptation to WRESTLE the knife away. Not only will you exhaust your energy rapidly, "wrestling" will cause excessive cuts to your hand. Your goal is NOT to overpower the attacker in order to take the knife away. Your goal is much simpler:

> **SAVE YOUR NECK** *(get the blade OFF your **AIR & BLOOD**)*
> **STOP attacker** *(destroy his **AIR**)*

RESIST trying to PULL THE ATTACKER'S *(knife-holding)* **HAND** off of your neck in an attempt to protect your hands from touching the blade. You are not likely to have enough power to pull his hand, arm (...and knife) away. It is not because of your size, but because *bar leverage* is against you! Your attacker can easily cut your neck in reaction to your *pulling motion* because *nothing* (like fingers) is between the blade and your throat, carotid artery or juggler vein.

It is good if the knife blade is LARGE ... because it will be easy to see and GRAB, greatly increasing your *bar leverage* to pull away the blade with ease.

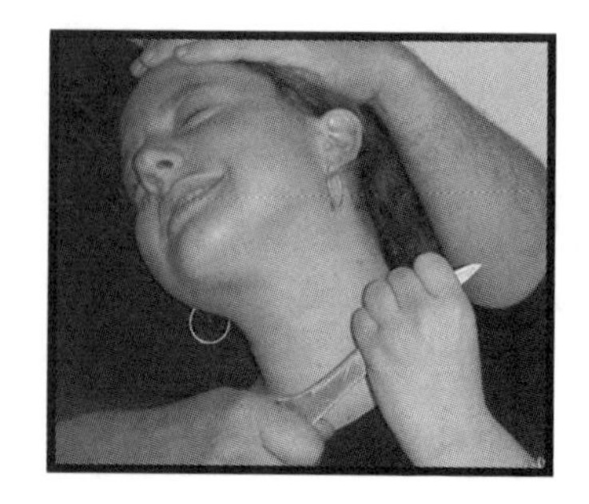

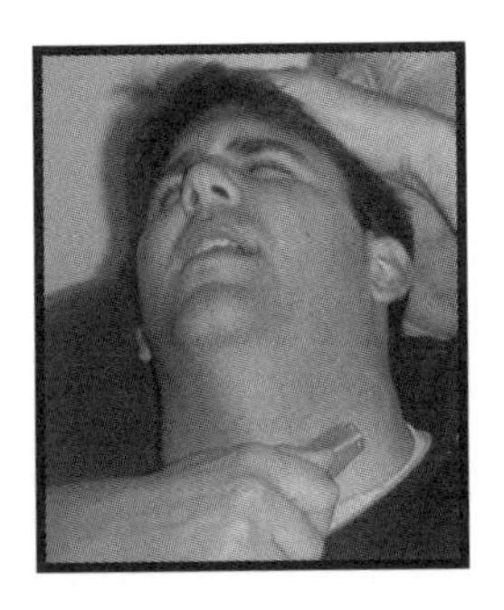

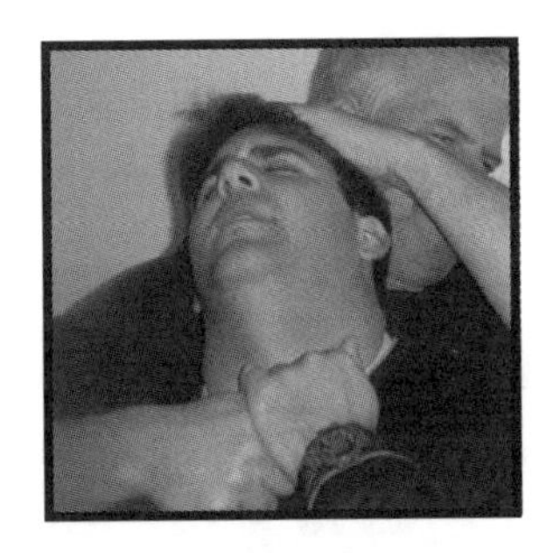

- A small knife or edged weapon is difficult *but not impossible* to GRAB and control.

  Box cutters, razors, pocketknives etc., are easily hidden in an assailant's hand and can be shoved rapidly against a throat with little to no warning.

Your defensive choices intensify:

☑ **DIG your fingers DEEPLY into your neck** behind the small blade. *Fight* for a solid GRIP!

☑ **PULL the blade away** from your neck to immediately save your AIR and BLOOD!

☑ **Strike the THROAT** to STOP the attacker's AIR

> If you think you "can" or you "can't", you're probably right!
>
> - Henry Ford

HOMEWORK:

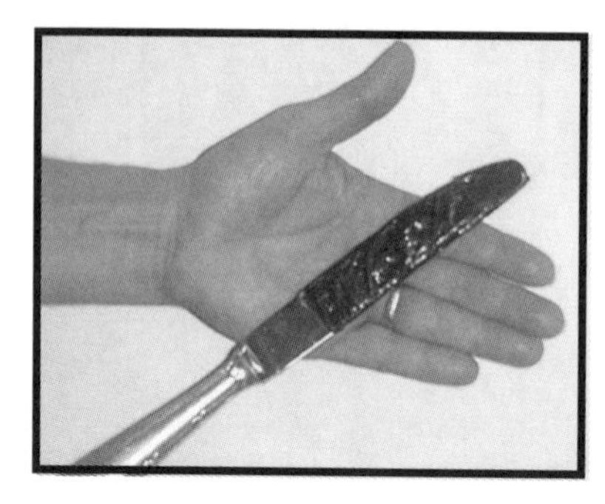

- Put a THICK layer of tape around a dinner knife to make sure the blade is safely covered.

- Ask a pretend-attacker to hold the knife by the handle while you grab the *taped* ***blade*** with force. Experience reality! The TIGHTER you GRIP the blade, the less the blade can move *(and cut)* your hand.

- Have your pretend-attacker put the *taped* ***blade*** at your neck. Try the WRONG CHOICE! Try to remove the blade by pulling the pretend attacker's *knife-holding* **hand and arm** off of your neck. *It is very difficult, isn't it?* Be ready for your pretend-attacker to brag: "I could have slit your throat!"

  Try it again. GRAB the *taped* BLADE and notice how simple *bar leverage* helps you ***easily*** pull the blade off your neck. Turn rapidly and imagine striking your pretend-attacker's THROAT!

  Are you stunned? *Bar leverage* blended with *courage* truly enhances your natural power!

  Ask your pretend-attacker to put a *magic marker* in your neck with force (simulating a box cutter, etc.) Experience how deep you need to dig your fingers behind that object to protect your neck. After securing a solid GRIP of the *pretend box-cutter* ... TURN and visualize hitting the THROAT!

KEEP YOUR BST "WEAPON SURVIVAL" PLAN SIMPLE ...
... JUST GRAB IT!

"I don't whether to take a gun defense class, knife defense class, stick defense class, bottle defense class, box-cutter defense class..."

Although guns and knives are usually a criminal's weapon-of-choice, ANYTHING (i.e., hammer, screw driver, baseball bat, golf club, chair, bottle, stool, etc.,) can be used as a WEAPON against you!

- ☑ **BREATHE/ROAR!** Grip! Visualize LOVED ONES!
- ☑ **PUT UP YOUR ARMS** in a *blocking surrender* position to protect your KILL ZONE
- ☑ **GRAB the *weapon*** (accept injury to your hand)
- ☑ **Strike the THROAT** to STOP the attacker

 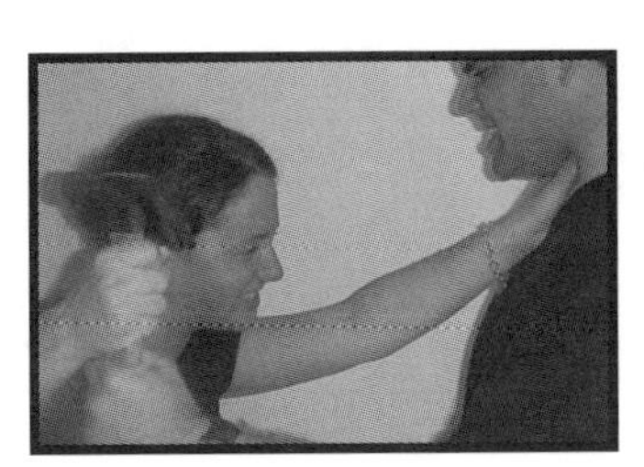 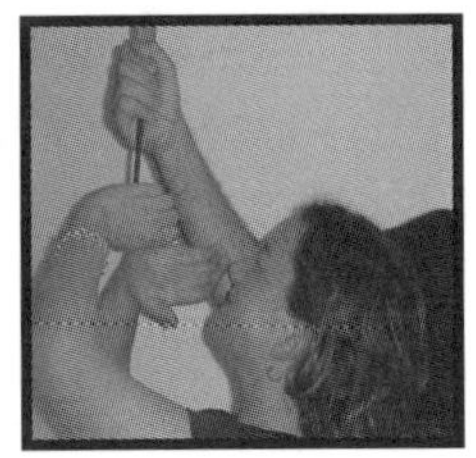

STRANGULATION

There are two methods an attacker can use to *strangle* his victim. He can use his arms/hands or a strangulation device such as a rope, electric cord, belt, stocking, etc. Assuming there was no chance to protect your space and hit the attacker ***first*** ... consider these options if strangled:

HAND/ARM STRANGLE

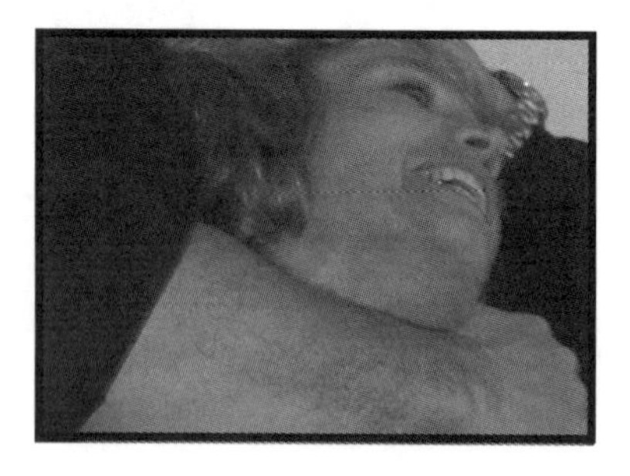

- ☑ **FIND AIR!** Struggle to move your THROAT to a spot that eases your sensation of *drowning*
- ☑ **BREATHE/ROAR!** Grip! Visualize LOVED ONES!
- ☑ **Bite him, twist his groin with your hands, or DO ANYTHING** within your reach to loosen his grip
- ☑ **Strike his THROAT** as soon as possible to STOP the attack. **RUN!**

STRANGLE DEVICES from behind

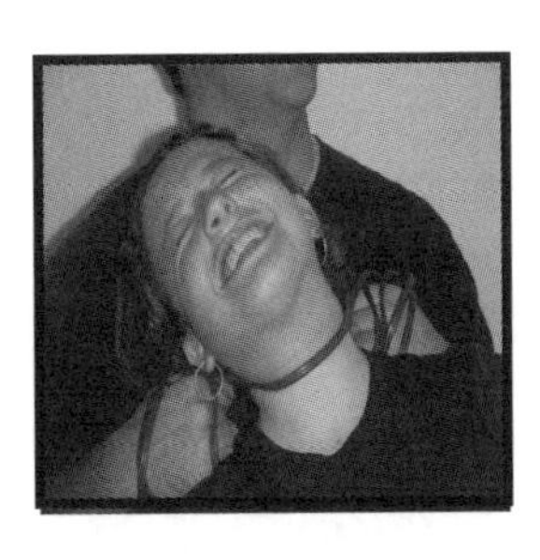

When testing *untrained* GOLDEN people, it is amazing how many try to reach up behind the strangulation device in an attempt to ease the pressure on their throat and pull the device away. This intensifies the strangulation!

The **BST** choice to survive strangulation is to:

☑ **TURN AROUND immediately** to reduce the concentrated pressure of a strangulation device on your AIR and BLOOD supply. There is nothing in the back of your neck to "strangle." Your windpipe, carotid artery and juggler vein are towards the front! It is possible that you will fall while turning ... no problem!

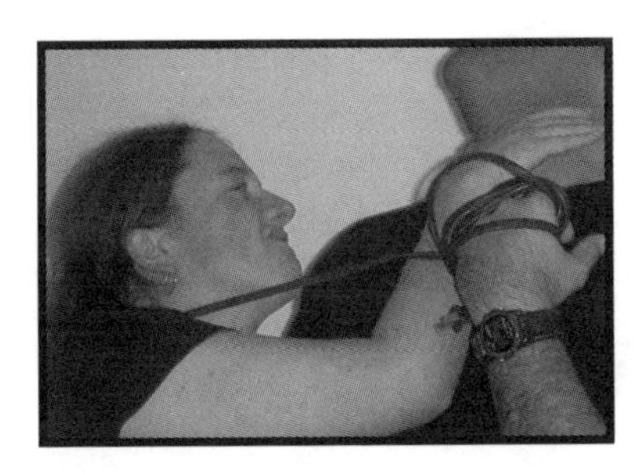

☑ **Strike the THROAT** quickly. The attacker's hands are *tied up* with the strangulation device. **RUN!**

Keep your **STRAGULATION SURVIVAL PLAN** SIMPLE!

Strangulation, like any smothering attack, is about ***oxygen:***

Fight to "FIND AIR" ... to save YOU!
Fight to "DESTROY AIR" ... to go home!

MULTIPLE ATTACKERS

When faced with more than one attacker, you are in serious danger. The odds are stacked against you. Assuming that options like *run* and *find help* are not possible *(which is usually the case)* ... be brave as you:

- ☑ **BREATHE!** Grip! Visualize LOVED ONES!
- ☑ **PUT your BACK against a wall, car, etc.,** to keep an attacker from getting you from ***behind***

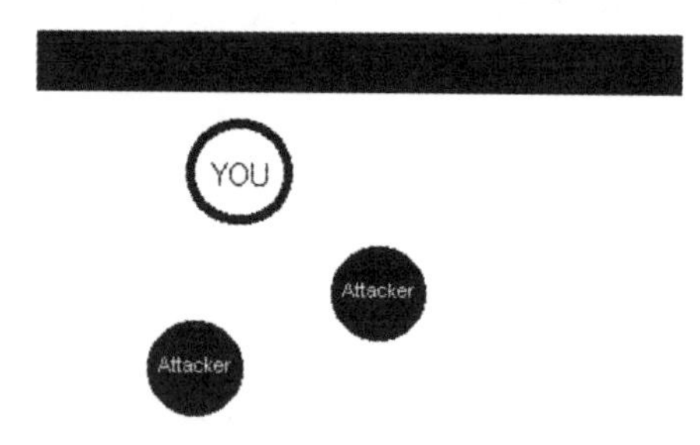

- ☑ **ASK, *"What do you want from me?"*** If they are thieves ... do not challenge them. A *gang* of thieves is a blessing compared to a *gang* of rapists or murderers.

    - **GIVE UP PROPERTY** immediately. Hopefully they are *happy* and leave!

- ☑ **CONFUSE ATTACKERS**. Make side-step movements to cause *them* to get in each other's way.

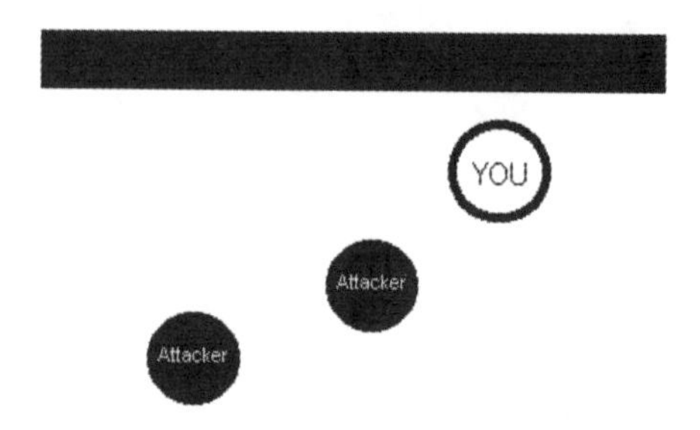

☑ Focus your attention on the ***leader*** (talker) especially if he is ***armed.***

☑ **Keep negotiating.** If he attacks:

- **GRAB and REDIRECT** the weapon

- **ROAR** to increase your confidence and intimidate your attackers. Roaring tightens your muscles, which increases your strength and protects your body from *feeling* many injuries. Also, someone *MIGHT* hear you!

- HIT the **leader's THROAT** ***first* ...** and other THROATS as they come in close.

If forced to defend yourself physically, remember you can only strike ONE attacker's THROAT at a time. Each strike needs to be effective because the odds of surviving are seriously against you. **DO NOT LIMIT YOUR OPTIONS WHEN FIGHTING MULTIPLE ATTACKERS.** Kick, bite, spit, pull hair, etc.

The **BST** strike when you can reach it is the **THROAT** because destroying AIR STOPS the attacker immediately! BE FEROCIOUS about defending your air which can easily be taken from behind by a criminal's swift grab at your ...

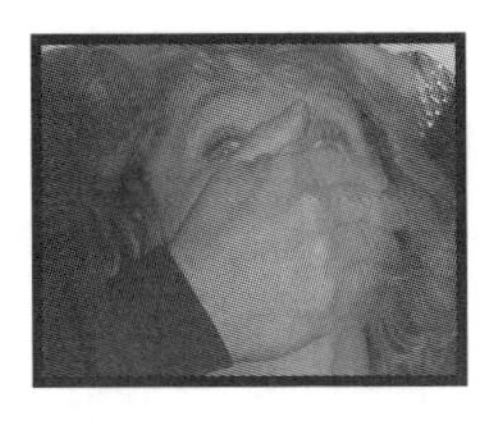

FACE and NOSE NECK CHEST

Remember, **you need AIR to fight!**

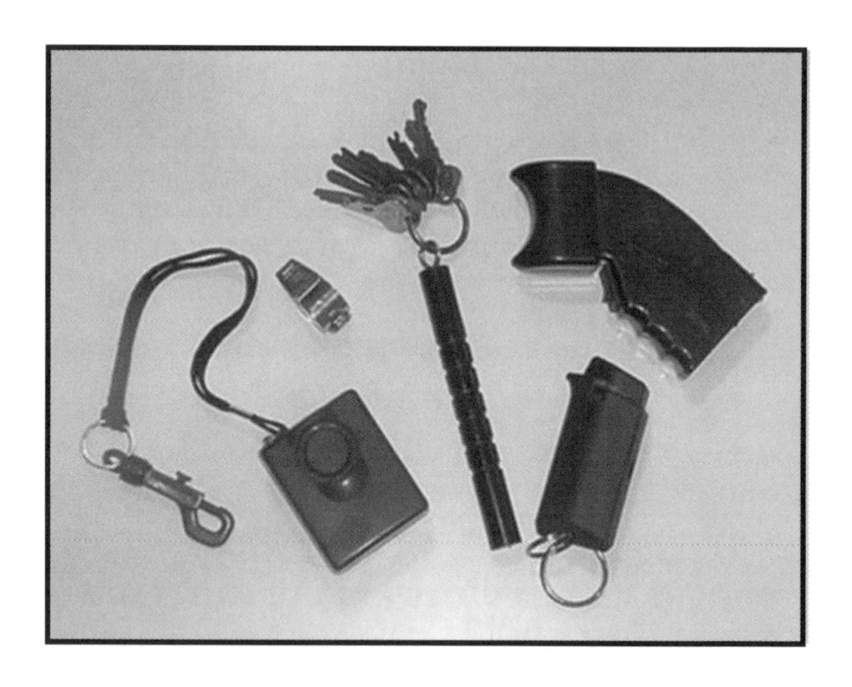

If only you could buy ... *guaranteed* safety and protection. Unfortunately a "perfect" self-defense product does not exist.

WEAPONS YOU CAN CARRY

I wish I had the nerve to sell a wide variety of self-defense products because I would be extremely wealthy by now. However, my conscious will not let me sell what I would never carry myself or encourage my family to carry. I categorize most self-defense/safety products as:

"MAYBE" PRODUCTS

... maybe they will work ... and maybe they won't.

CHEMICAL SPRAYS

I remain unimpressed with the **STOPPING** power of chemical sprays (any brand, any size). Yes, I know that police carry chemical sprays. They also carry *batons* and *guns* when sprays fail to STOP violent behavior. I know some brands have more of an eye irritation and/or choking effect than others, but here is my problem. Where is the **manufacturer's guarantee** that attackers who are **drugged, enraged or intoxicated will STOP** vicious violence because their breathing and eye sight is impaired? Here are other "maybe" issues:

- *Maybe* the product is on, *maybe* it's off
- *Maybe* the contents are new, *maybe* old
- *Maybe* it streams 5 feet, *maybe* 5 inches
- *Maybe* it hits his eyes, *maybe* his chin

If your ONE HIT delivered by a self-defense spray *angers* ... rather than *stops* ... an enraged attacker, then you are in double-trouble! **Remember, the BST crime survival plan encourages you to cause *injury*, not just pain.** If an attacker continues to fight you, the chemical spray may cause *you* to experience chronic vision and breathing impairment because you *feel* the irritation and the attacker does not.

In my opinion, the only valuable part of a pepper spray or chemical irritant is the CANISTER! Use it as a *handle* on your keys to GRIP when you are afraid. Faced with unpreventable violence:

☑ **THRUST** the chemical spray CANISTER into the attacker's THROAT to STOP him!

SOUND/SHREIK ALARMS

"Maybe" sound alarm products are not good enough for me or my family.

- *Maybe* the attacker will be scared off by the noise, and *maybe* he won't!
- *Maybe* people will hear ... and help and *maybe* they won't!
- *Maybe* the battery is dead and *maybe it isn't*!

If you are desperate and have a sound alarm in your hand ... chose a guaranteed injury:

☑ **THRUST** the alarm **BOX** into the attacker's THROAT to STOP him!

NEVER expect to be saved by others.
Expect only to save yourself!
Help from someone who hears you struggle, is a ***BONUS!***

WHISTLES

Whistles are ridiculous for self-defense. Whistles require AIR to make noise. In true terror, air is not flowing freely in your neck and chest. In a crisis, I am convinced that wrapping lips around a whistle and blowing is all but impossible for most people.

In a crisis, you are more likely to *swallow* a whistle ... than *blow* one. Besides, who *really* responds to the sound of a whistle blowing? I would recommend that you use your precious AIR to **ROAR** for benefits described in Chapter 5!

GUNS or KNIVES

The choice to carry a gun or knife for self-defense is quite personal. Remember that a gun or knife is only useful if it is *in your hands* and ready to use at the time of an attack. Check your state laws.

CELL PHONES

Cell phones are priceless! Because cell phones are so affordable, I look forward to a time when *everyone* has communication in their pocket or purse. Program your cell phone for **9-1-1 rapid dialing.**

When frightened, GRIP you cell phone, and dial 9-1-1. Give your **LOCATION FIRST** ... then describe your circumstance. Follow your **BST** plan. If an attacker charges at you:

☑ **THRUST the phone** into the THROAT!

Cell phones are especially valuable if your car breaks down. You can control *who* comes to your rescue. Other unique products that contribute to your safety when driving are products like OnStar™ and other GPS (global positioning satellite) products.

If you are a *road warrior,* traveling all hours of the day and night, I strongly encourage you to invest in the added protection of OnStar™ or other GPS products! In an emergency, your car can be *located* and *tracked* by satellite!

Car trouble is annoying and can be dangerous! If you do not have access to a cell phone, CB, OnStar™ or GPS system ... you are at the mercy of "strangers" to help you.

"SEND POLICE" CAR BANNER

A large, florescent car banner that reads "SEND POLICE" is a very inexpensive alternative to cell phones and GPS systems for travel safety. Buy one that has *suction cups* which makes the sign "re-useable" and will adhere to your rear car window regardless of *hot* or *cold* outdoor temperatures.

"SEND POLICE" banners alert all passing vehicles to LOOK at you and ... "SEND the police." Many will dial 9-1-1 for you.

> If traffic is heavy, **police will come quickly** because the dispatcher will be irritated with all the calls coming in reporting your condition. (The banner secretly becomes an *irritate the police dispatcher* sign...OOPS!) Anyway, your broken-down car will become a police *priority!*
>
> **Criminals** *(who can read)* **are intimidated** by SEND POLICE signs. It makes them think that the police are *on their way.* Odds are a potential criminal will just drive past you ... even if you are on an isolated road.

CAR SAFETY with NO PRODUCTS

If your car is broken down, and assistance is not within safe walking distance, you need to control yourself and get ready to "interview/test" a stranger who may stop to "help."

You need to use clever, verbal tools to identify that ***one**-in-a-million* stranger who might ***pretend*** to help you, but actually intends to harm you.

A car has just pulled up behind your car. A man is walking towards your window. Your heart is pounding ...

☑ **BREATHE!** Grip! Visualize your LOVED ONES!
☑ **LOCK** your doors
☑ **WAIT** until he is at your window. **Then, ROLL down your window just a few inches.** *This well-timed and awkward action sends this message:* ***I don't trust you!*** *A reasonable person will understand and not be offended!*

☑ **TALK FIRST ... LOUDLY** (a sign of confidence!)
With RED fire-eyes, say something GOLDEN like this:

... *THANK YOU for stopping*
... *You are the SECOND person to stop* ***(this is a lie)***
... *A man left 10 minutes ago* ***(lie)***
... *He called the police, they're on their way* ***(lie)***
... ***Would you LEAVE and CALL POLICE AGAIN?*** **(test!)**

A TRUSTWORTHY person will LEAVE ... and probably call the police. You'll never really know. What's important is the stranger *listened* and followed your instructions!

An UN-TRUSTWORTHY person will STAY ... and argue with you. He will pretend to *care* about you and your car. He will say all kinds of things that sound reasonable in an attempt to get into your *space* and/or *lure you* out of your car ... into his vehicle. EXAMPLE:

"Show me how to open the hood so I can check your engine."
"Well, I can drive you to the repair shop ..."

☑ **DO NOT LEAVE YOUR LOCKED CAR!** If he truly cares about your safety ... he will listen to you! Repeat your firm commands:

> ... *No! Don't check my engine.*
> ... *NO! I don't want a ride to* ______
> ... *LEAVE and call the police... NOW!*

If you are forced to repeat "LEAVE and call the police" THREE TIMES:

☑ **ROLL UP YOUR WINDOW** immediately
☑ **BLOW YOUR HORN** until he goes away

You would be safer sitting there for another hour ... waiting for a stranger who *listens* and stays out of your space ... then take a chance with someone who thinks he knows what you need, better than *you know* what you need.

Your "car" may be broken-down ... but not your "courage!"

> "... And what the heart KNOWS today the head will understand tomorrow."
>
> Unknown

KEYS

Keys are with us everyday, making them very valuable for self-dense applications. Years ago, it was common to teach: *"Put your keys between your fingers and 'rake' your attacker's face."* Years ago, attackers could ***feel*** rakes across their face. Times are different now! Criminals today often ***feel* nothing** at the time they attack.

Faced with unstoppable violence, make your keys dangerous:

☑ **Thrust ONE KEY** into an attacker's THROAT!

Better than that, put a "handle" on your key ring. Choose something that gives you a comfortable GRIP. Gripping keeps you're *ready* without thinking about being *ready* (like the GRIP of your steering wheel keeps you ready to avoid an auto accident.) Put a "handle" on your keys that is *larger* than your hand (five or more inches) so that **either end** of the object can be used as a weapon to:

☑ **Thrust HANDLE** into an attacker's THROAT!

Examples of "handles" for your keys: flashlight, wrench, or what I and all my family and friends carry ... a KUBOTAN!

KUBOTAN®

The KUBOTAN® was invented by Master Takayuki Kubota for police officers to use as a pain compliance tool useful in controlling criminal suspects. I used it quite successfully in my "road patrol" days.

KUTOBANS are valuable self-defense tools for civilians, too. There are many reasons why Mike and I have carried a KUBOTAN consistently for 25 years and have encouraged our family to do the same:

... **"GRIPPING" feels good** ... especially when afraid! Gripping the KUBOTAN enhances the circulation of blood and oxygen in your body, especially when you feel ***the creeps.***

... KUBOTANS are hard to lose. Measuring 5 ½ inches in length (about the size of a magic marker) KUBOTANS fit nicely in briefcases, purses, and pockets, making keys easy to find in a hurry.

... IT LOOKS TOUGH! Maybe this sounds corny, but people look at a KUBOTAN and *respect* it! Unlike keychain-style chemical sprays, thousands of police and civilian **men** as well as women carry KUBOTANS. When you GRIP it, you stand tall and *act ready...* because you are!

... IT IS AN EFFECTIVE WEAPON! In a worse-case scenario, either end of the KUBOTAN is an injury-causing weapon when used to strike the throat!

... KUBOTANS are CHEAP and LAST FOREVER! A KUBOTAN is a one-time-purchase product that costs about the same as a fast-food meal! KUBOTANS do not *expire* like chemical sprays and do not require batteries like sound alarms and stun guns. I am presently carrying a black KUBOTAN that an elderly woman carried for 19 years! She bought it after seeing our first TV interview in the early 80's! She attended a recent seminar and raved about the courage her KUBOTAN gives her when she GRIPS! Due to her failing eyesight, I was happy to trade a new white KUBOTAN for her old black one. It is in perfect condition!

In a violent attack, it is likely you will strike an attacker ***faster*** with a KUBOTAN (or any object) ... than with just your *naked* hand. Some people admit they are likely to **hesitate** at the thought of touching a criminal, skin to skin.

For this reason, I *strongly* encourage you to put some type of "handle" on your keys immediately. If you ever feel the ***creeps*** and your keys are not available, pick up and GRIP anything close, like a cell phone, beeper, water bottle, TV remote, brush, stapler, etc.

If nothing is available to GRIP, please understand that your **BST** tools are your **bare hands** because...

... You can't leave home without them!

WEAPON SURVIVAL SUMMARY

When *desperate* and *trapped*, your life-saving options are limited. Decide that ***you*** *(not the attacker)* will choose which part of your body is injured!

- ☑ **BREATHE/ROAR!** Visualize LOVED ONES
- ☑ **GRAB** and **redirect** the weapon from your KILL ZONE!
- ☑ Strike the **THROAT**. **RUN!**

Strangle	TURN	Find AIR	Strike THROAT
Gun	**GRAB** Barrel	Redirect	Strike **THROAT**
Knife	**GRAB** Blade	Redirect	Strike **THROAT**
Box-cutter	**GRAB** Blade	Redirect	Strike **THROAT**
Hammer	**GRAB** End	Redirect	Strike **THROAT**
Screwdriver	**GRAB** End	Redirect	Strike **THROAT**
Bottle	**GRAB** End	Redirect	Strike **THROAT**

The **ONE** word summary that **BST** describes most weapon defenses is **GRAB.** It requires *courage!*

PRACTICE by watching violence on TV and at the movies. Watch the right and wrong choices *movie stars* make as they *pretend* to survive weapon violence. While *wrestling* for a gun, where is the barrel (bullet) aimed? During an abduction scene, is a large knife hanging past the heroin's neck? Is the victim hysterical or breathing deeply for control?

In the state of *Hollywood created fear* ... decide if a GRAB of the gun BARREL or knife BLADE would be a more realistic choice ... for YOU! This *emotional practice* is priceless programming to incorporate your new, **BST** beliefs into your everyday life. Remember it is your **WILL-power** (attitude) that needs repetitious practice, more so than you *muscle* power and practice of techniques.

KEEP YOUR BST
"WEAPON SURVIVAL" PLAN
SIMPLE!

Chapter Eight

Celebration of Courage

Imagine the privilege of *standing up for something bigger than yourself!* Imagine creating true, positive impact in someone else's life. Imagine actually *saving* a life someday.

These are not lofty dreams. Starting today, turn those imagined images into everyday realities! Armed with new ideas you've learned in this book, teach others to STAND UP for their 24-hour **RIGHT to LIVE,** free of excessive fear! Insist that if they **LOVE**, they have access to **MVP** power on command! Give them **permission** to follow their dreams without fearing crime with every step they take ... *alone.* Teach the life-saving meaning of **BST** and give them encouragement to **GRAB weapons** for KILL ZONE protection.

Join me in my private quest to transfer the **attitude** of ***limited freedom*** from law-abiding citizens ... to criminals.

Yes, I am *stubborn* in my belief that:

MOST *people ...*
MOST *the time ...*
can at least **TRY** ...
to **save their own life** ...
with **simple** principles...
they **believe** they can do!

ADVICE FOR "HEALERS" of BROKEN HEARTS

Immediately after a loved one has survived a crime, any crime, please stay *physically* close *with your mouth taped shut* as long as he/she needs you! Keeping your opinions to yourself during this crucial time will require great discipline.

LISTEN with LOVE. No lectures! No commentary! Just nod you head "Yes" with *love* in your eyes. Listen carefully.

Imagine your survivor in a place called **emotional intensive care!** Your job as healer is to shield *your patient* from all ***verbal viruses*** that visitors and family members might bring in. Careless visitors can make your patient even more (heart) sick!

When you feel your patient has gained enough strength, speak with great discipline, offering this comment FIRST ...

"In a similar situation, I hope I could be half as ______ (brave) as you. You truly inspire me." ... Then, BE QUIET!

"**LESS is MORE**" when verbally supporting crime survivors. A survivor's ears are like *radar*, listening for negative judgment. The most innocent word or phrase will be interpreted as a *stab of guilt* to someone in **emotional intensive care**! Saying, *"I'm sorry"* or *"Oh, I didn't mean it that way"* doesn't help. There are NO VERBAL ERASERS!

When others assure you they will NOT infect your survivor with *verbal viruses*, encourage them to visit if they *listen* a lot and *speak* a little ... using at least one of these words in every sentence:

Brave	Fearless	Strong	Amazing
Courageous	Awesome	Hero	Fantastic
Noble	Righteous	Incredible	Fabulous
Spectacular	Proud	Inspiring	Remarkable

SUPERCALIFRAGILISTICEXPIALIDOCIOUS! *(Mary Poppins)*

AVOID talking on the phone around your survivor. Repeated descriptions of the crime details will cause irritation. No matter what you say, your version will not be completely accurate.

Discuss "updates" privately with police, nurses, doctors, lawyers, etc. Remember, "...what you focus on, EXPANDS!" When a survivor is in **emotional intensive care** their heart needs to focus on *celebration, love* and *gratitude* to accelerate healing of their body, mind and heart!

> With a steady diet of *verbal vitamins* and the passage of time, your survivor's heart will begin to heal and their emotional foundation will firm-up from *quicksand* to ***concrete.***

> Remember the old saying: "What doesn't kill us ... makes us strong!" I like it except for the fact it doesn't mention the need to find the *right* path towards strength and healing. The *wrong* path, loaded with *negative people and verbal viruses*, can be described this way: "What doesn't kill us immediately ... just destroys us slowly."

Buy a personal GIFT for your survivor. Choose something that can be touched or seen often. Memorize ONE beautiful sentence to say when giving the gift. Your *gift of words* will reach the heart. Your *gift of jewelry* will reach the hand. Consider saying something like:

"I am so incredibly PROUD of YOU. I LOVE YOU..."

Then, BE QUIET! ***Silence is GOLDEN*** especially when combined with tears of gratitude, joy and love. These tears are tremendous healing medication for *both* your hearts.

> I have come to understand a powerful observation. Crime survivors receive something from everyone who encounters them after an attack. That *something* creates *negative or positive* impact! *"Something given"...*

usually starts with the letter **"G"** ... and appears in the form of **G**IFTS (positive) or ... **G**UILT (negative)!

Help me teach people to exchange their old habit of giving *accidental guilt* (judgment) ... to a new habit of giving *deliberate gifts* (celebration). **Celebration gifts** are *positive* energy. **Judgmental guilt** is negative energy. A survivor's HEART cannot equally accept both *gifts* and *guilt* (positive and negative feedback) over the same event.

Think of physical and verbal GIFTS as **bullet-proof vests** that will help insulate and protect your survivor's heart from judgmental stabs and bullets!

Carefully introduce HUMOR. Have a funny TV show, video or DVD ready to watch with the survivor. **ASK** if laughter would be OK! Sit close. Make sure no *crime scenarios* are in the story line.

Sponsor a CELEBRATION PARTY when your survivor is out of *emotional intensive care* and is ready to **try** to get back to normal. Keep the energy lighthearted. Be as clever as you can with fun themes and gags to keep your survivor and party goers laughing and hugging. It doesn't have to cost a lot of money, it will cost a lot of **time** and **love...**

It is an enormous job to be a BROKEN-HEART "HEALER." Take good care of yourself during this difficult time because you have been technically attacked too, in a very different way. Keep this thought in mind: "You can only *give* ... what you *have!*" Think of your face as a mirror. If you show hope, your survivor will **see *hope***. If you show peace, your survivor will **see *peace***. I did not say your survivor... *will have hope and peace,* I said SEE hope and peace. You are the first *path of light* that leads your loved one in the direction they need to go for healing.

Whenever you are *low,* remember the ***power of prayer*** as you seek wisdom and meaning behind your loved one's experience with senseless human brutality.

ADVICE FOR BROKEN-HEARTED SURVIVORS

A ***contented heart*** *is the greatest blessing*
a person can enjoy in this world.
Joseph Addison

You are the reason I do what I do. I'm bothered by your *private suffering* and am determined to find the missing piece that has the power to lead you to rapid recovery and a *contented heart.* I'm wondering if I made a discovery? Is a big reason you are still *suffering* after all this time because you haven't yet had a:

"I SURVIVED!" PARTY?

Whether you have been beaten, abducted, raped, bullied, verbally abused, emotionally abused, stolen from, shot, stabbed, tricked, stalked, threatened or set-on-fire ... is it possible that those who love you forgot to publicly CELEBRATE what you did right ... **YOU *PREVENTED* — MURDER!**

GOLDEN people love to celebrate birthday parties, retirement parties, holiday parties, anniversary parties, graduation parties ... why not CRIME SURVIVAL PARTIES? What is a *bigger accomplishment* than preventing death?

FORGIVE your loved ones! When it comes to crime issues, GOLDEN people are NOT programmed to see and celebrate the positive. They do not know to send out party invitations, bake a cake, hang up the decorations, and buy you gifts. The word *celebration* doesn't cross their mind!

> NO! GOLDEN people are programmed to review details of your attack and then offer you advice and behavior changes so that this ***never*** happens again. They are suffering *with* you and *for* you, which just makes you feel worse. *Group whispers* are everywhere ... because *groups* are not sure what to say to your face, although you can imagine what they are saying

your back. Loving, meaningful communication, at the time you need it most, is non-existent because everyone is tip-toeing around!

Maybe your well-meaning loved ones and friends have *accidentally* given your heart the *opposite* of what it needs:

GUILT instead of **GIFTS!**

THROW YOURSELF A PARTY! WASTE NO MORE TIME! Parties have "healing power". Do for yourself what you can no longer wait to have done for you! A public ***CELEBRATION*** is your missing piece. It can cost less than one *therapy* session. Set up an opportunity for everyone to *talk about it* with the *expert* ... YOU. Your heart will instantly be *patched.* You'll be on the road to true healing after an evening filled with *validating* words of awe, respect and courage from those who truly love you.

> Negative, guilt-oriented judgment will not occur at your party because you are going to BE BOLD and take control of the party atmosphere by clearly printing these words on your invitation:

"ONLY POSITIVE ATTITUDES are welcome!"

Talk to any "cancer survivor" and they will tell you that the surgery and chemo was important, but what *really got them through* their life and death crisis was the flood of positive communication ... cards, gifts, flowers, candy, etc., in addition to genuine, encouraging heart-talk from *everyone* in their life! Many had *parties* too!

Are you so low that the idea of a big party overwhelms you? Then start small. Celebrate *your* survival, *by yourself* if you must!

Eat a nice meal, put a candle on a store-bought cupcake and focus on all that obviously went *right* that day. **Then open up a GIFT you bought *yourself!*** This is important! Buy something that you can wear or see daily as a reminder *of your courage!* **Be in awe of YOU!**

> Any gift will work but I like to recommend **jewelry** ... *GOLDEN* jewelry for a *GOLDEN* survivor! If your attack involved a weapon ... buy GOLD jewelry with DIAMONDS! Depending on the size of your wallet, you can buy ***real*** or ***fake*** jewelry. I don't care. I just want your heart to feel good and heal ... NOW!

Your gift will become a visual reminder of your courage and serve as an attention-getter that others will see and compliment. I suggest you respond to a compliment this way:

> *"Thank you, yes this is a nice _________(bracelet, ring, golf club, etc.) I bought it for myself in celebration of SURVIVING an extraordinary event in my life."*
>
> It is not important to tell them the details of your *survival*, just the details of your growth and *celebration!*

HANG OUT with "balcony people" those who pull you *up* by respecting and acknowledging your *expertise.*

STAY AWAY from "basement people" those who pull you *down*! Have you ever seen a "statue" erected in honor of ... a *critic*?

FILL YOUR MIND AND HEART with words of wisdom that make you feel good.

This is a sample ... one of my favorite:

The MAN in the ARENA

It's not the critic who counts. Not the one who points out how the strong person stumbled or how the doer of the deeds might have done them better.

The credit belongs to the person who is actually in the arena; whose face is marred by blood, sweat and dust, who strives valiantly but errs and comes short again and again because there is no human endeavor without shortcoming; who knows the great enthusiasms – the great devotions, and who; if he wins ... knows the triumphs of high achievement **and who, if his efforts are checkered by defeat ... at least fails while daring greatly so that his place shall never be with those cold and timid souls ...who know neither VICTORY nor DEFEAT!**

Teddy Roosevelt – 1899

Write or email me! I want to benefit from your wisdom! I'm just a self-defense *teacher* ... **YOU are the *expert!*** That's right ... expert! You and other crime survivors have massive wisdom if we can just get you all to open up, get you past the fear of undeserved judgment and shame, and tell us what you *really thought* and *did* that ... prevented murder!

FINALLY, I want to leave you with a simple suggestion that will *profoundly* heal your heart ... if you choose to apply it:

"HAPPINESS" *is the **BeST revenge!***

Happy people drive *unhappy people* CRAZY! **When you refuse emotional poison, it becomes even worse in the sender, but not in you!**[1] Live with peace, love and happiness everyday. And, you are allowed to *fake it* ... until you make it!

[1] Don Miguel Ruiz, *The Four Agreements*

PERSONAL FREEDOM for ALL!

People *assume* I am in the *self-defense* business. That is not exactly accurate. I am in the ***FREEDOM Business*** and use self-defense as my path to reach people!

I am thankful for years of feedback from participants who successfully used my **BST** message to help them prevent a crime or save their own life in all kinds of challenges, not just crime survival. One of my favorite success stories involves no blood, no criminals, no police. It involves something bigger, the rebirth of personal ***FREEDOM.***

A retired woman came early to a seminar I was conducting in Toledo, Ohio. She caught my eye and asked if I had time to talk privately. I was *stunned* by her comments:

*"Debbie, I just want to tell you that my **lifetime dream** came true because I came to see your seminar **last** year!"*

"I'm a retired nurse. I always dreamed about buying a new car, and driving out West when I retired. I'm single, no kids, never married. I used to volunteer to work extra shifts on holidays so my colleagues could be with their families. To fight loneliness, I would daydream about retirement ... bumping along Route 66, with no schedule, just enjoying the scenery and the people as I go."

"So, when I retired, I bought a new car, then told my friends at Card Club about my dream. I was sure that someone would want to go with me"

*"The ladies in my Card Club shattered my dream. They thought I was out of my mind for even thinking about such a trip. One friend actually said, **'People like us CAN'T do something like that. We are too old. Someone will take advantage of us.'"***

"So, I got to thinking that the way things are these days, she was probably right and I was probably wrong. Then I started to wonder about somebody taking advantage of me ... here in Toledo, especially at night. Before long, I was afraid to do just about everything. I got so depressed sitting in my condo all day."

"I saw an ad for your seminar in the paper and I decided, even though it was scheduled across town at night time, I was going to go and learn something to snap out of my misery. Well, I left so 'fired up' believing in my 'rights' again and knowing I could do it ... I could BREATHE and hit THROATS in a crisis ... that you will not believe what I did?"

She paused, then continued with an enormous smile on her face: *"I DID IT! I drove out West this past summer. I drove along Route 66 for two weeks ... **BY MYSELF**!"*

> *"You really did that?"* I asked. I remember being amazed, not just by her story, but by her glowing facial expressions.

*"YES I DID! And ... I am driving **back** this summer for THREE weeks with my friend that I want you to meet. I insisted that she come here to learn your self-defense and feel good about her RIGHTS too!" Like me, she is sick of living with all the fears seniors put on themselves and each other!"*

> *"Oh my goodness,* I said. *"You are an inspiration to me. I want to be just like you when I grow up and retire!"*

I talked to her friend. We all hugged. Then, I just had to ask her a dangerous question:

> *"Please be honest, were you ever afraid? Did you have any close-calls or **feel the CREEPS**?"*

"NO! Not a single incident. I looked everybody in the eyes. Hey, I was a nurse! You reminded me that I know how to control people. I had the time of my life. I made friends that I am anxious to visit again this summer. My new car worked beautifully. I bought a cell phone like you recommended and sent away for one of your 'car signs' and 'grippers' and I have pictures you would not believe! I can't wait to go back....so THANK YOU!"

"NO! Thank you! You have made my day!" I told her.

A more accurate comment would have been *"you have made my career!"* This adventurous, brave and inspiring senior citizen is ALIVE again! LIVING her dreams again! HEALTHY again ... because she adjusted her *fear of crime.*

Even though she was close to 70 years old, she dared to believe that if ***something happened***, she could apply the **BST** plan to handle it, just as she handled medical emergencies all those years as a nurse. Her confidence was back! She would be the first to tell you she did not make *careless* choices, but she did make *reasonable* choices to see *new* things and meet *new* people. Some people call that *risk.* She calls it *living.*

Inspired by this incredible woman's determination and courage to fulfill her lifetime dream *alone*, Mike and I drove home that night feeling as if we earned "success" equivalent to a GRAMMY or an OSCAR! Although we suspect there are others who we have *set free*, we know **for sure** that there is ONE ... in Toledo, Ohio.

Years ago, as young police officers, Mike and I came home troubled by the pain of victimization and *fear of crime* we witnessed regularly. We dared to dream: "***maybe by designing something different, something outrageously simple, we can make a difference in people's lives!"*** According to our retired, senior citizen friend in Toledo, our lifetime dream has come true ... in partnership with hers!

Some people live ... DYING.
Others die ... LIVING!

SENIORS: I am not encouraging you to live *carelessly* and take *extreme risks* just because you know the **BST** plan. I am encouraging you to decide to *live* fulfilling your dreams. R*easonable risks* are potentially everywhere, every second, everyday ... exactly as they have been your whole life.

You are not *a beginner* in the "risk-taking, problem-solving department!" Even though you might walk a little slower, you still have decades of life skills to draw upon. Decide *who* has the right to define *risk* for you and thereby design the rest of your life ... *You* or someone else? If anyone deserves freedom, it is you, for all the sacrifices you have made (i.e., Depression, World Wars, etc.) to make this Country great!

TEENAGERS: Do not take my passion for personal FREEDOM out of context. If you are under 18 years of age, your personal freedom is *limited.* As a minor, you are subject to the laws, rules and restrictions of your community, school and **parents.**

Once you journey out on your own as a *new* adult ... REMEMBER: 100% of *all risks* you take are 100% your *responsibility* even though you have little or no experience. It is because you are a *beginner in adult responsibility* that your parents want you to be extra careful to *limit* the number of risks you take until you become *street-smart!* They already know, and you are about to find out, it is no one's responsibility *to solve your adult problems, pay your bills or even save you in a violent crisis* ... but YOURS! They know "freedom" is not FREE ... of *risk* and *responsibility.*

> EXAMPLE: You have always wanted to swim across the river. You are a good swimmer. You technically have the right to try. Swimming across a river is something society generally thinks is **risky**. You know it is more risky for some people than others. You know *you* can do it.
>
> If you act upon your risky dream with a well thought out **plan** (i.e., a life vest, a boat following you, etc.) you will probably succeed, or at least *live.* You'll earn bragging rights and can enjoy celebrating the thrill of your physical accomplishment for years.
>
> If, however, you act upon your risky dream with no **plan ...** because you reacted impulsively to a friend's *dare* late at night while drinking beer on the shore ... you'll probably *fail* and maybe *die.* Yes, you had the right and *freedom* to try, but you took a risk without a reasonable **plan ...** and ultimately paid with consequences ... that destroy your parents' heart.

PARENTS: Raising kids is tough! Here is the problem. Kids want to be free to take *risks* but you know they do not *see* and therefore do not *accept responsibility* if something goes wrong. They want to *blame* someone else then have you "*fix it*" as soon as possible. They do not understand the *risk/ responsibility* partnership. Do you want your children to be safe? Then, BE FIRM starting now! Let them suffer the *consequences* of their *risky choices!*

For your children's safety decision making skills *later* STOP putting a pillow under their butt every time they fall *now.*

How can you expect your children to master the art of *weighing risk* at age 16 ... *(the most dangerous age of their life ... because they are new at dating and driving)* if they have been protected from the consequences of poor choices all their childhood?

> Example: If your 10 year-old smashes his mouth because he chose to skateboard down 25 concrete steps ... Be CALM (Breathe deeply and GRIP something.) Be THANKFUL! This is a chance to teach a wonderful lesson about *risk and responsibility!*
>
> Give no hysterical *I told you so...* lectures. He doesn't need *guilt*, he needs *consequences*. Knowing he is in pain, but not in a life-threatening situation... give him extra time to think and suffer as you drive calmly, NOT RUSHING ... to the doctor.
>
> NO RESPONSE ... is a response! Shock him by controlling your *verbal* reaction. Calm, quiet, controlled responses from you will *scare* your kid more than the *expected* lecture! Read magazines in the waiting room. Let HIM tell the doctor what happened. Let him be *frightened* by the doctor's needles ... his own *blood* ... and your *calmness.*
>
> On the drive home, you do not need to talk much. Give him quiet time to decide, at age 10, if the *painful* consequences (and *financial consequences* if you ask him to help pay a portion of the medical expenses) were worth his *high-risk choice (THRILL)* of skateboarding down concrete steps.
>
> If the *consequences* were painful and severe enough, (in his opinion, not yours) he will adjust his level of risky behavior ... *skateboarding down steps...* and in other inevitable high-risk choices down the road!

SPOUSES: It is important that you extend the "assumption" to your mate that *either of you* can handle a violent crisis effectively. It would be helpful if you both agreed on the same **(BST)** plan! Of course, it is nice for women when the men of the house embrace the role of *defender!* Most women love that! The problem is, designated *male defenders* are not always around when women need them!

Ladies, it is nice to "be taken care of" but your husband needs to know that you can *switch hats* and equally take care of yourself in his absence! When married partners create the habit of expressing *worry* and *doubt* about each other's abilities, especially over *safety* issues, feelings are hurt and marital *friendships* are damaged. Verbal support and respect of each other's personal freedom is a great vitamin to strengthen marriages.

> EXAMPLE OF SWITCHING HATS:
> When traveling, Mike prefers to be the driver of our car. He is in charge of my safety and his. I enjoy being taken care of and relaxing when he drives. However, when he is not around, I am FREE and capable of driving my car safely by myself. Mike knows I have driving skills EQUAL to his. I appreciate that he does not *worry* or *doubt* my ability to drive safely ... *OR walk alone in a parking lot!*

SINGLES: *Independence* is your middle name! Congratulations if you have found comfort being *alone* and *trusting yourself* with all decisions in your life. Acknowledge that testing and trusting "strangers" is a big part of your life; therefore, danger is often hidden in your shadow. You will not know if you can *trust* a potential mate or new friend, until you *trust* that potential mate or friend. Perhaps your confidence has been damaged in the past because your trust was violated. Do not look back in *anger,* or forward in *fear,* but continue to look around in *awareness* ... backed-up by my **BST** plan.

FINAL THOUGHTS

As a gift for completing this book, I want to lend you my *title* ... **Most *Dangerous* Woman in America,** whenever you need it! (*Of course men will want to drop off the "Wo...!"*)

I made up this title for **us** to publicly declare a spirit and attitude that has the power to save lives! *Our title* is not about being cocky, obnoxious or arrogant. In fact, we are quite the opposite. *Our title* reflects our belief that in a crisis, for our LOVED ONES, we can do anything ... or at least TRY!

Most people are about as
dangerous, *loving, and happy ...*
as they make up their minds to be!

Debbie Gardner

"My parents are the *nicest*
and *scariest* people I know."

Jaclyn Gardner

Like me, you can be **dangerous** on command, not because you are motivated by anger or hatred, but because you are motivated by LOVE. This unique self-defense principle is long overdue! Enjoy your GOLDEN life knowing that you can become an effective defender by turning *RED* for *LOVE ONES* in an instant. Isn't it ironic that:

People paint symbols of LOVE ...
with the same color
as anger and hatred
... RED!

SUMMARY of "*Simply the BST Crime Survival*"

When Mike and I dreamed about designing a simple self-defense plan *that MOST people could use effectively, MOST of the time, with little or no practice,* we dreamed of it being so simple that it could fit on the *back* of our business card.

We exceeded our goal! Our self-defense message is THREE LETTERS (three words) that you WILL **NOT** FORGET:

BST

B = BREATHE!
S = SPACE
T = THROAT

Thank you for **GRAB**bing this book, it's life-saving message, a powerful new title ... (and **weapons** if you are desperate!)

I beg you to help me create a *revolution* in self-defense education by teaching my **BST** plan to other **MVP's!** Crush cardboard "tubes" with emotion and excitement every chance you get knowing that you are now an **empowered** member of the largest *street gang* in America ...

GOLDEN PEOPLE!

About the Author

Debbie retired from the Hamilton County (Cincinnati) Sheriff's Department after 8 years employment as a Deputy Sheriff. She was one of the first women in the United States to be assigned patrol duty, *alone,* in the mid 70's. She was certified by various national and international self-defense training programs along with her husband, Mike, a 27 year veteran of the Cincinnati Police Department. Mike is presently the training commander (Captain) of the Warren County Sheriff's Office in Ohio.

Debbie is the author of ***SURVIVE! Don't be a Victim***, published by Warner Books (New York). She is the creator of a Corporate Safety Training Video series entitled ***YES YOU CAN! Surviving a Personal Attack*** (Curtis Inc., Cincinnati OH) as well as, ***YES YOU CAN!*** a two hour family video. Debbie was acknowledged as America's #1 Female Crime Fighter in the premier issue of Crime Fight magazine. She has been the subject of feature articles in magazines and newspapers throughout the United States and Canada, including *Vogue* and *Cosmopolitan.* She has also been the guest on numerous national television shows. She just completed ***SURVIVE with Debbie Gardner*** a "Pledge Special" for Public Television.

Debbie founded the Survive Institute in 1982 as the result of 7,000 letters she received immediately after a regional TV appearance. The host convinced her she had a responsibility to share her "gift" of teaching *fear control* and *courage* in her unique way.

Debbie and Mike have conducted their revolutionary crime survival seminars and workshops for hundreds of corporations, conventions, and colleges in almost every state in the US and in Canada, South America, Australia and Europe. Some of their clients include: General Motors, Procter and Gamble, Kelly Services, Ford, and Young Presidents Organization. They are members of the National Speakers Association.

Learn More About Survive Institute

Retreats, Seminars, and Training Programs

Debbie Gardner conducts seminars and workshops for conventions, business, universities, hospitals, schools, and law enforcement agencies. She also conducts full day, hands-on classes for groups such as: teacher in-services, security services, law enforcement officers, business offices, etc.

Debbie also provides "Courage Coaching" Houseboating Retreats on Lake Cumberland, Kentucky for individuals, families or groups.

For more information on trainings and seminars, call 513-791-7453 or write to:

Survive Institute
7265 Kenwood Road, Suite 315
Cincinnati, Ohio 45236
You can also visit her web site:
www.surviveinstitute.com

Books, Tapes and other Items

Additional copies of this book and other items listed below are offered by the Survive Institute.

Simply the BST Crime Survival Book	$ 15.95
KUBATON Keychain (Grip Keychain)	$ 5.95
SEND POLICE Car Banner	$ 5.95
Yes You Can! Family Video (2 hours)	$ 34.95
Yes You Can! Corporate Video Series (including facilitator's guide)	$395.95

Quick Order Form

FAX orders: 513-791-7453. Send this form.
TELEPHONE orders: call 513-791-7453
EMAIL orders: debbiegardner@surviveinstitute.com.
POSTAL orders: Survive Institute
7265 Kenwood Road, Suite 315
Cincinnati, Ohio 45236 USA

Please send me the following items ...

____ **$** __________

____ **$** __________

____ **$** __________

Shipping & Tax **$** _________

TOTAL **$** _________

Please send me more information about:

Seminars Physical Classes "Courage Coaching" Retreats

Name: ____

Address: ____

City: _________________________ State: ____ Zip: ____________

Telephone: (_____) _________________________

Email Address: _________________________________

Sales Tax: Please add 6.00% for products shipped to Ohio.

Shipping and Handling Charges:
US: $4 for the first item and $2 for each additional product.
International: $9 for the first item and $5 for each additional product (estimate).